LIGUORI CATHOLIC BIBLE

The Gospel
of Luke

SALVATION FOR ALL HUMANITY

WILLIAM A. ANDERSON, DMIN, PHD

Liguori
LIGUORI, MISSOURI

Imprimi Potest:
Harry Grile, CSsR, Provincial
Denver Province, The Redemptorists

Printed with Ecclesiastical Permission and Approved for Private or Instructional Use

Nihil Obstat:
Rev. Msgr. Kevin Michael Quirk, JCD, JV
Censor Librorum

Imprimatur:
+ Michael J. Bransfield
Bishop of Wheeling-Charleston [West Virginia]
April 2, 2012

Published by Liguori Publications
Liguori, Missouri 63057

To order, call 800-325-9521
www.liguori.org

Library of Congress Cataloging-in-Publication Data
Anderson, William Angor, 1937-
   The Gospel of Luke : salvation for all humanity / William A. Anderson. --
1st ed.
     p. cm.
   1. Bible. N.T. Luke--Textbooks. I. Title.
   BS2596.A53 2012
   226.4'06--dc23
                              2012022446
p ISBN 978-0-7648-2122-6
e ISBN 978-0-7648-6724-8

Liguori Publications, a nonprofit corporation, is an apostolate of the Redemptorists. To learn more about the Redemptorists, visit Redemptorists.com.

Printed in the United States of America
16 15 14 13 12 / 5 4 3 2
First Edition

Contents

NOTE: The length of each Bible section varies. Group leaders should combine sections as needed to fit the number of sessions in their program.

ACKNOWLEDGMENTS

Bible studies and reflections depend on the help of others who read the manuscript and make suggestions. I am especially indebted to Sister Anne Francis Bartus, CSJ, DMin, whose vast experience and knowledge were very helpful in bringing this series to its final form.

This series is lovingly dedicated to the memory of my parents, Kathleen and Angor Anderson, in gratitude for all they shared with all who knew them, especially my siblings and me.

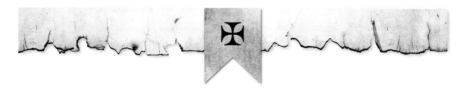

Introduction to
Liguori Catholic Bible Study

READING THE BIBLE can be daunting. It's a complex book, and many a person of goodwill has tried to read the Bible and ended up putting it down in utter confusion. It helps to have a companion, and *Liguori Catholic Bible Study* is a solid one. Over the course of this series, you'll learn about biblical messages, themes, personalities, and events and understand how the books of the Bible rose out of the need to address new situations.

Across the centuries, people of faith have asked, "Where is God in this moment?" Millions of Catholics look to the Bible for encouragement in their journey of faith. Wisdom teaches us not to undertake Bible study alone, disconnected from the Church that was given Scripture to share and treasure. When used as a source of prayer and thoughtful reflection, the Bible comes alive.

Your choice of a Bible-study program should be dictated by what you want to get out of it. One goal of *Liguori Catholic Bible Study* is to give readers greater familiarity with the Bible's structure, themes, personalities, and message. But that's not enough. This program will also teach you to use Scripture in your prayer. God's message is as compelling and urgent today as ever, but we get only part of the message when it's memorized and stuck in our heads. It's meant for the entire person—physical, emotional, and spiritual.

We're baptized into life with Christ, and we're called to live more fully with Christ today as we practice the values of justice, peace, forgiveness, and community. God's new covenant was written on the hearts of the people of Israel; we, their spiritual descendants, are loved that intimately by God today. *Liguori Catholic Bible Study* will draw you closer to God, in whose image and likeness we are fashioned.

Group and Individual Study

The *Liguori Catholic Bible Study* series is intended for group and individual study and prayer. This series gives you the tools to start a study group. Gathering two or three people in a home or announcing the meeting of a Bible-study group in a parish or community can bring surprising results. Each lesson in this series contains a section to help groups study, reflect, pray, and share biblical reflections. Each lesson also has a second section for individual study.

Many people who want to learn more about the Bible don't know where to begin. This series gives them a place to start and helps them continue until they're familiar with all the books of the Bible.

Bible study can be a lifelong project, always enriching those who wish to be faithful to God's Word. When people complete a study of the whole Bible, they can begin again, making new discoveries with each new adventure into the Word of God.

Lectio Divina
(Sacred Reading)

BIBLE STUDY isn't just a matter of gaining intellectual knowledge of the Bible; it's also about gaining a greater understanding of God's love and concern for creation. The purpose of reading and knowing the Bible is to enrich our relationship with God. God loves us and gave us the Bible to illustrate that love. As Pope Benedict XVI reminds us, a study of the Bible is not only an intellectual pursuit but also a spiritual adventure that should influence our dealings with God and neighbor.

The Meaning of *Lectio Divina*

Lectio divina is a Latin expression that means "divine or sacred reading." The process for *lectio divina* consists of Scripture readings, reflection, and prayer. Many clergy, religious, and laity use *lectio divina* in their daily spiritual reading to develop a closer and more loving relationship with God. Learning about Scripture has as its purpose the living of its message, which demands a period of reflection on the Scripture passages.

Prayer and *Lectio Divina*

Prayer is a necessary element for the practice of *lectio divina*. The entire process of reading and reflecting is a prayer. It's not merely an intellectual pursuit; it's also a spiritual one. Page 14 includes an Opening Prayer for gathering one's thoughts before moving on to the passages in each section. This prayer may be used privately or in a group. For those who use the book for daily spiritual reading, the prayer for each section may be repeated each day. Some may wish to keep a journal of each day's meditation.

Pondering the Word of God

Lectio divina is the ancient Christian spiritual practice of reading the holy Scriptures with intentionality and devotion. This practice helps Christians center themselves and descend to the level of the heart to enter an inner quiet space, finding God.

This sacred reading is distinct from reading for knowledge or information, and it's more than the pious practice of spiritual reading. It is the practice of opening ourselves to the action and inspiration of the Holy Spirit. As we intentionally focus on and become present to the inner meaning of the Scripture passage, the Holy Spirit enlightens our minds and hearts. We come to the text willing to be influenced by a deeper meaning that lies within the words and thoughts we ponder.

In this space, we open ourselves to be challenged and changed by the inner meaning we experience. We approach the text in a spirit of faith and obedience as a disciple ready to be taught by the Holy Spirit. As we savor the sacred text, we let go of our usual control of how we expect God to act in our lives and surrender our hearts and consciences to the flow of the divine (*divina*) through the reading (*lectio*).

The fundamental principle of *lectio divina* leads us to understand the profound mystery of the Incarnation, "The Word became flesh," not only in history but also within us.

Praying *Lectio* Today

Before you begin, relax your body and maintain a posture of prayer (back straight, eyes shut, feet flat on the floor). Then practice these four simple actions:

1. Read a passage from Scripture or the daily Mass readings. This is known as *lectio*. (If the Word of God is read aloud, the hearers listen attentively.)

2. Pray the selected passage with attention as you listen for a specific meaning that comes to mind. Once again, the reading is listened to or silently read and reflected or meditated on. This is known as *meditatio*.

3. The exercise becomes active. Pick a word, sentence, or idea that surfaces from your consideration of the chosen text. Does the reading remind you of a person, place, or experience? If so, pray about it. Compose your thoughts and reflection into a simple word or phrase. This prayer-thought will help you remove distractions during the *lectio*. This exercise is called *oratio*.

4. In silence, with your eyes closed, quiet yourself and become conscious of your breathing. Let your thoughts, feelings, and concerns fade as you consider the selected passage in the previous step (*oratio*). If you're distracted, use your prayer word to help you return to silence. This is *contemplatio*.

This exercise can take as long as you want, but in the context of this Bible study, 10 to 20 minutes should be sufficient.

Many teachers of prayer call contemplation the prayer of resting in God, a prelude to losing oneself in the presence of God. Scripture is transformed in our hearing as we pray and allow our hearts to unite intimately with the Lord. The Word truly takes on flesh, and this time it is manifested in our flesh.

How to Use This Bible-Study Companion

THE BIBLE, along with the commentaries and reflections found in this study, will help participants become familiar with the Scripture texts and lead them to reflect more deeply on the texts' message. At the end of this study, participants will have a firm grasp of the Gospel of Luke and realize how that gospel offers spiritual nourishment. This study is not only an intellectual adventure, it's also a spiritual one. The reflections lead participants into their own journey with the Scripture readings.

Context

When the author wrote his gospel, he didn't simply link random stories about Jesus—he placed them in a context that often stressed a message. To help readers learn about each passage in relation to those around it, each lesson begins with an overview that puts the Scripture passages into context.

Part 1: Group Study

To give participants a comprehensive study of the Gospel of Luke, the book is divided into ten lessons. Lesson 1 is group study only; Lessons 2 through 10 are divided into Part 1, group study, and Part 2, individual study. For example, Lesson 2 covers passages from Luke 2:1 through 4:13. The study group reads and discusses only Luke 2:1–52 (Part 1). Participants privately read and reflect on Luke 3:1 through 4:13 (Part 2).

Group study may or may not include *lectio divina*. With *lectio divina*, the group meets for ninety minutes using the format at the top of page 12. Without *lectio divina*, the group meets for one hour using the format at the bottom of page 12, and participants are urged to privately read the *lectio divina* section at the end of Part 1. It contains additional reflections on the Scripture passages studied during the group session that will take participants even further into the passages.

Part 2: Individual Study

The gospel passages not covered in Part 1 are divided into three to six shorter components, one to be studied each day. Participants who don't belong to a study group can use the lessons for private sacred reading. They may choose to reflect on one Scripture passage per day, making it possible for a clearer understanding of the Scripture passages used in their *lectio divina* (sacred reading).

A PROCESS FOR SACRED READING

Liguori Publications has designed this study to be user friendly and manageable. However, group dynamics and leaders vary. We're not trying to keep the Holy Spirit from working in your midst, thus we suggest you decide beforehand which format works best for your group. If you have limited time, you could study the Bible as a group and save prayer and reflection for personal time.

However, if your group wishes to digest and feast on sacred Scripture through both prayer and study, we recommend you spend closer to ninety minutes each week by gathering to study and pray with Scripture. *Lectio divina* (see page 7) is an ancient contemplative prayer form that moves readers from the head to the heart in meeting the Lord. We strongly suggest using this prayer form whether in individual or group study.

GROUP-STUDY FORMATS

1. Bible Study With *Lectio Divina*

About ninety minutes of group study

- ✠ Gathering and opening prayer (3–5 minutes)
- ✠ Scripture passage read aloud (5 minutes)
- ✠ Silently review the commentary and prepare to discuss it with the group (3–5 minutes)
- ✠ Discuss the Scripture passage along with the commentary and reflection (30 minutes)
- ✠ Scripture passage read aloud a second time, followed by quiet time for meditation and contemplation (5 minutes)
- ✠ Spend some time in prayer with the selected passage. Group participants will slowly read the Scripture passage a third time in silence, listening for the voice of God as they read (10–20 minutes)
- ✠ Shared reflection (10–15 minutes)
- ✠ Closing prayer (3–5 minutes)

To become acquainted with lectio divina, *see page 7.*

2. Bible Study

About one hour of group study

- ✠ Gathering and opening prayer (3–5 minutes)
- ✠ Scripture passage read aloud (5 minutes)
- ✠ Silently review the commentary and prepare to discuss it with the group (3–5 minutes)
- ✠ Discuss the Scripture passage along with the commentary and reflection (40 minutes)
- ✠ Closing prayer (3–5 minutes)

Notes to the Leader

✠ Bring a copy of the *New American Bible,* revised edition.

✠ Plan which sections will be covered each week of your Bible study.

✠ Read the material in advance of each session.

✠ Establish written ground rules. (Example: We won't keep you longer than ninety minutes; don't dominate the sharing by arguing or debating.)

✠ Meet in an appropriate and welcoming gathering space (church building, meeting room, house).

✠ Provide name tags and perhaps use a brief icebreaker for the first meeting; ask participants to introduce themselves.

✠ Mark the Scripture passage(s) that will be read during the session.

✠ Decide how you would like the Scripture to be read aloud (whether by one or multiple readers).

✠ Use a clock or watch.

✠ Provide extra Bibles (or copies of the Scripture passages) for participants who don't bring their Bible.

✠ Ask participants to read "Introduction: The Gospel of Luke" (page 15) before the first session.

✠ Tell participants which passages to study and urge them to read the passages and commentaries before the meeting.

✠ If you opt to use the *lectio divina* format, familiarize yourself with this prayer form ahead of time.

Notes to Participants

✠ Bring a copy of the *New American Bible,* revised edition.

✠ Read "Introduction: The Gospel of Luke" (page 15) before the first class.

✠ Read the Scripture passages and commentaries before each session.

✠ Be prepared to share and listen respectfully. (This is not a time to debate beliefs or argue.)

Opening Prayer

Leader: O God, come to my assistance,

Response: O Lord, make haste to help me.

Leader: Glory be to the Father, and to the Son, and to the Holy Spirit...

Response: ...as it was in the beginning, is now, and ever shall be, world without end. Amen.

Leader: Christ is the vine and we are the branches. As branches linked to Jesus, the vine, we are called to recognize that the Scriptures are always being fulfilled in our lives. It is the living Word of God living on in us. Come, Holy Spirit, fill the hearts of your faithful, and kindle in us the fire of your divine wisdom, knowledge, and love.

Response: Open our minds and hearts as we study your great love for us as shown in the Bible.

Reader: (Open your Bible to the assigned Scripture(s) and read in a paced, deliberate manner. Pause for one minute, listening for a word, phrase, or image that you may use in your *lectio divina* practice.)

Closing Prayer

Leader: Let us pray as Jesus taught us.

Response: Our Father...

Leader: Lord, inspire us with your Spirit as we study your Word in the Bible. Be with us this day and every day as we strive to know you and serve you and to love as you love. We believe that through your goodness and love, the Spirit of the Lord is truly upon us. Allow the words of the Bible, your Word, to capture us and inspire us to live as you live and to love as you love.

Response: Amen.

Leader: May the divine assistance remain with us always.

Response: In the name of the Father, and of the Son, and of the Holy Spirit. Amen.

The Gospel of Luke

Read this overview before the first class.

When a teenager asked his grandfather what book he was reading these days, the grandfather said, "I'm reading a book about my life." The youth, enthused that his grandfather would have a book written about himself, asked anxiously, "What's the name of the book?" The teenager laughed when his grandfather responded, "It's called the Bible!"

Although the Bible is the Word of God, it is not only about God and God's dealings with the people of the past; it is also a collection of stories about us. As we understand the Bible more fully, we will understand its application to our lives.

The Historical Climate

After Jesus ascended into heaven, his followers thought they would continue to live as faithful Jews who believed the Messiah had come in the person of Jesus, with the expectation that all Jewish people would eventually accept that belief. Little did Peter and the other disciples realize at the time that the followers of Christ would eventually be rejected by the Jewish leadership of the era and become a faith apart from Judaism. Christianity would gain a far greater number of converts from among the Gentiles than among the Jews. Gentile Christian communities sprouted up rapidly in areas outside Jerusalem.

In time, Paul the Apostle became the Apostle of the Gentiles. Paul recognized the difficulties encountered by Gentiles in attempting to live a faith that had its roots in Jewish laws and customs. Guided by the Holy Spirit, Paul eventually convinced the leadership of Jewish Christian converts that the Gentiles should not be obligated to follow Jewish dietary laws and customs, but ought to be free to follow the message of Christ in a manner familiar to their culture. After many years of struggle and confrontation, the Gentiles were eventually able to live as faithful followers of Christ without the burden of Jewish dietary laws and customs. Paul was beheaded around 64, and approximately twenty years later, the author of the Gospel of Luke penned a gospel addressed to Gentile believers in the Christian Way.

Who Was Luke?

Like other gospel writers, the author of the Gospel of Luke fails to identify himself. By studying the style and cultural traits of this gospel, we can gain some insight into the author's background, but we must look toward later writings to discover the author's name. In reading the gospel, we can assert that the author was a Gentile Christian who lived outside of Palestine and, according to most commentators, seems to be a Syrian from Antioch. He has a perfect grasp of the Greek language and its classical usage, and he shows a greater knowledge of the world of Asia Minor than he does of Palestine.

The author omits the extensive use of Old Testament prophecies as found in the Gospel of Matthew. He shows his great literary skills when he declares in his opening statement that his aim is to present "in an orderly sequence" the gospel so that the reader may "realize the certainty of the teachings" presented.

An early third-century catalog of the books of the New Testament, known as the Muratorium Fragment, names Luke as the author of this gospel. The Muratorium Fragment apparently had some authority in Rome around the year 200, and it states that the author of the Gospel of Luke also wrote the Acts of the Apostles. Another ancient writer named Irenaeus, who wrote around the same period in which the Muratorium Fragment was written, also names Luke as the author of this gospel. Although other writers support this view, the Muratorium Fragment and Irenaeus are the earliest writings to identify Luke as the author. Despite the evidence of ancient writings that identify Luke as the author of the gospel, a question still remains, namely: Who was Luke?

Besides this early evidence, similarities between the Gospel of Luke and the Acts of the Apostles point to the same author for both books. The opening lines of both writings address a certain "Theophilus" as the recipient of the book, and Acts speaks of a previous book about Jesus Christ. The Acts of the Apostles begins where the Gospel of Luke ends. With this evidence, some look to the Acts of the Apostles to discover the identity of Luke. The evidence seems to point to a companion of Paul as the author of this gospel and the Acts of the Apostles, but the evidence is weak and inconclusive.

In his letters, Paul does speak of a companion named Luke, who is later identified as "the physician" (2 Timothy 4:11; Colossians 4:14). Al-though the author of the Acts of the Apostles never gives his own name, the author identifies himself as a companion of Paul the Apostle in Acts 16:10–17, where he uses the term "we," as though he, Paul, and others traveled together. Many commentators find this use of "we" inconclusive, since it could be a literary device used to strengthen the author's writing, or it could be the author's use of a source from another writer who traveled with Paul. Although no one is certain about the true identity of the author of this gospel, we will refer to him as Luke throughout the following pages.

Who Was Luke's Audience?

While Matthew wrote for converts from Judaism, Luke wrote for converts from among the Gentiles. Matthew presents Jesus as a true Israelite whose ancestry reaches back to Abraham, the father of the Israelite nation. Wish-ing to show Jesus in a more universal light, Luke traces Jesus' family line back to Adam, the first human mentioned in the Bible. As stated above, he addresses his gospel to "Theophilus," a Greek, non-Jewish name. Luke writes not only for those outside Judaism but also for all outcasts: the poor, the sick, sinners, women, foreigners, and conquerors. He writes a gospel filled with compassion and mercy for the downtrodden.

When Was the Gospel of Luke Written?

The Gospel of Luke was written somewhere between 80 and 90. Since the author uses Mark as one of his sources, we must assume the Gospel of Mark had some time to become known and accepted within the early Church. Mark wrote his gospel about the year 70. Luke, like Matthew, shows a clearer knowledge of the destruction of Jerusalem than Mark does. The destruction of this great city took place in 70, which gives further evidence that the author wrote his gospel after this well-known event in Jewish and Christian history.

No evidence shows that Matthew or Luke had any knowledge of the other's gospel, though both used another written source commonly referred to as "Q" by modern Scripture scholars. The letter comes from the first letter of the German word *Quelle,* which means "source." Luke, like Matthew, is also said to have had an oral source that came to him from his community, from which he drew some passages not found in the other gospels.

What Are Some Characteristics of Luke's Gospel?

Mark develops an image of Jesus also incorporated in the Gospels of Matthew and Luke, since they both use Mark as one of their sources. (See The Synoptic Problem in the introductory book of this series, *Introduction to the Bible.*) As a result, many of the characteristics of Mark's Gospel will appear in the Gospels of Matthew and Luke, but they will sometimes be used to emphasize a different message than the applications made by Mark. In investigating how the Gospels of Matthew and Luke apply the Gospel of Mark, the reader can better understand the purpose of Matthew and Luke in writing their gospels and how their use of Mark shows the difference between the Gospel of Matthew and that of Luke. (See Redaction Criticism in the introductory book of this series). Matthew uses Mark as his source almost twice as much as Luke does.

Jesus as a Universal Savior

A major characteristic of the Gospel of Luke is that it was written for all people. As insignificant as this might sound today, it was most significant for the early Church, as at that time many people from all nations were accepting the teachings of Jesus Christ.

How did Jesus, a Jew, show his concern for all people, and what right did others outside of Judaism have to accept Jesus as their savior? Luke answers these questions by placing Jesus at the center of creation rather than at the center of the Jewish faith. The Gospel of Luke continually reminds the reader that the Good News is to be brought to the entire world, and not only to the Israelites. Jesus is the savior of all creation.

Concern for the Outcast

In Luke's story of the birth of Jesus, we immediately catch a glimpse of the direction of the gospel. The weak shepherds (not the wise Magi of the Gospel of Matthew) pay homage to Jesus. In Luke's Gospel, Jesus shows concern for the poor, the sinful, the rejected Samaritans, the sick, and women. To the Jewish mind of Jesus' day, the people comprising these groups were the outcasts and downtrodden of society. At best, they were the second-class citizens of the day.

Jesus' Journey Toward Jerusalem and His Death

Luke introduces us to Jesus and his ministry in the first part of the gospel and dedicates the second part to detailed events of the long journey of Jesus toward Jerusalem. The message tells us that Jesus knew of his destiny and followed the will of God to the end. It was fitting for Jesus, the great prophet, to die in Jerusalem, the place where many of the prophets of the past faced their death. The gospel ends with the final triumph of Jesus' resurrection in Jerusalem and a short summary of the Ascension of Jesus. (A more detailed version of the Ascension can be found at the beginning of the Acts of the Apostles, which explains how the message of Jesus spread from Jerusalem to the whole world.)

A Spiritual Gospel

Luke emphasizes the place of prayer in Jesus' life. Before important events in his life, Jesus goes off by himself to pray. The Spirit becomes very active in the life of Jesus. And the true lover and disciple of Jesus is the one who abandons all material goods for the sake of God. Luke calls his readers to spiritual surrender and complete trust in a loving God.

The Structure of the Gospel

At the beginning of his gospel, Luke promises that he will present a well-ordered narrative of the life of Jesus and his message from the material gained from other witnesses. The structure fulfills the promise of the writer who wrote, "I too have decided, after investigating everything accurately anew, to write it down in an orderly sequence for you…so that you may realize the certainty of the teachings you have received (1:3–4).

Prologue: Infancy Narrative

LUKE 1:1–80

"My soul proclaims the greatness of the Lord; my spirit rejoices in God my savior. For he has looked upon his handmaid's lowliness; behold, from now on will all ages call me blessed" (1:46–48).

Opening Prayer (SEE PAGE 14)

Context

Luke's Gospel begins by explaining that he has gathered material for his gospel from "eyewitnesses" (1:2). The narrative opens with the Annunciation and Nativity stories of both John the Baptist and Jesus, presenting a parallel between both births. Luke informs us that Zechariah and Elizabeth are the parents of John and that the Virgin Mary conceives Jesus through the power of the Holy Spirit.

Luke's Gospel is the only synoptic gospel that has a prologue. The author of the gospel writes in the style typical of Hellenistic Greeks, thus relating his message about Jesus to the current Greek and Roman writers of the era.

PART 1: GROUP STUDY (LUKE 1:1–80)

Read aloud Luke 1:1–80.

1:1–4 Luke gathers his sources

At the beginning of his gospel, Luke states that others have written about the events that have taken place in their midst, and he admits that he is not an eyewitness to the message he is about to deliver. Instead, he has gathered his material to present an orderly message to his readers. He writes about the person and message of Jesus Christ as preached by the members of the early Church. The original message came from those who were eyewitnesses to Jesus and his preaching.

When Luke speaks of presenting his message in an orderly form, he does not mean the events that follow occurred precisely as they did in Jesus' life. In writing his gospel, he follows the order of many of the events found in the Gospel of Mark and adds the sayings of Jesus (the written "Q" source) to the oral tradition passed on by those known to Luke. Matthew also makes use of some of the sayings of Jesus used by Luke, but he places them in a position in his narrative that fits the theme of his gospel. The order chosen by Luke is for the sake of his message and is meant to emphasize that Jesus came for the salvation of all humanity. Matthew wrote his gospel for Jewish converts to Christianity, whereas Luke wrote for all people, particularly the Gentile converts.

Luke addresses his letter to Theophilus, which means "beloved of God." This dedication may refer to some benefactor or early Christian convert who was considered by members of the early Church as someone close to God. In classical writings of the time, addressing a letter to someone important or held in high esteem was a common practice. This custom did not mean the letter was meant for that person alone. Luke intended this gospel for all people, and some commentators believe that the title "Theophilus" was a name meant to include all those who were "beloved of God." Luke also wrote the New Testament book of the Acts of the Apostles, and he begins Acts by again addressing "Theophilus" and making reference to his "first book," which is his gospel.

1:5–25 Annunciation of the birth of John the Baptist

In the infancy narrative (the second section of Luke's Gospel), the author writes flawless Greek, indicating that he was a well-educated Gentile who was dependent on the Greek Septuagint. (See *Introduction to the Bible*, book one of the *Liguori Catholic Bible Study*.) Since the infancy narrative contains a style of Greek that differs from the rest of the gospel, it is likely the work of an independent author incorporated into this gospel by Luke.

Matthew and Luke are the only gospels to include an infancy narrative, but they differ so drastically that neither of them could have known the sources used by the other. Both of these writers present the infancy narrative as a type of overture for the rest of the gospel. Thus, many of the events found therein foreshadow the conflicts Jesus will encounter during his life. Though they may not have happened as presented, the reader must keep in mind that this is an inspired message about Jesus, not an historical or scientific analysis of events. Matthew structures his gospel to show that Jesus is the fulfillment of the Old Testament prophecies, so he explicitly quotes from the Old Testament, showing how Jesus fulfilled these prophecies. Luke is less explicit and subtly includes allusions to the Old Testament in the narrative itself.

Luke's narrative is carefully structured to show a parallel between the annunciation and birth of John the Baptist and that of Jesus, focusing on Jesus as the greater of the two. The other gospels will stress the importance of Jesus over John, but they emphasize this when John baptizes Jesus. Luke presents a narrative about the annunciation of the birth of John, directly followed with a story about the annunciation of the birth of Jesus. After the annunciation stories, he presents a narrative about the birth of John, followed by the birth of Jesus. In doing this, he is using a literary form to show a parallel and link between the two births.

The infancy narrative begins within the historical confines of Judea, identifying King Herod as the Roman ruler of Judea. By placing his narrative within the context of history, Luke is able to develop his theme of universal salvation for all. He situates the annunciation of John's birth within the context of Jewish history by naming Herod the ruler of Judea.

Zechariah, a priest, and his wife, Elizabeth, a descendant of Aaron, are introduced as a holy couple dedicated to the Law of God. They both belong to priestly families. Elizabeth was elderly and barren, a plight common to certain significant women of the Old Testament who gave birth to important children. The barren womb of Elizabeth brings to mind women such as Sarah, who gave birth to Isaac (Genesis 21:3); Rebekah, who gave birth to Jacob and Esau (Genesis 25:25–26); Rachel, who gave birth to Joseph (Genesis 30:22–24); and Hannah, who gave birth to Samuel the prophet (1 Samuel 1:20). The people of Israel viewed barrenness as a curse from God.

Luke uses images from the story of the birth of Samuel, found in the opening chapters of 1 Samuel in the Old Testament. Hannah, the mother of Samuel, is barren, and she begs God to free her from this curse. God heard her prayer, and she gave birth to Samuel. Like Hannah, Elizabeth was barren and advanced in years, making a birth seemingly impossible. With the announcement of the birth of John the Baptist, the angel frees Elizabeth from the curse of her barrenness. Luke stresses trust in God by presenting impossible situations and showing how God intervenes.

When Luke speaks of the events surrounding the visitation of an angel, he follows a standard format used for heavenly visitations found throughout the Old Testament. Such visitations are usually received with fear, and the angel responds with comforting words, announcing some outcome to the visit. The person receiving the vision replies that the outcome is impossible, and the angel responds with some sign that the promised event will take place.

Zechariah is in the Temple sanctuary offering incense when an angel appears to him. He is the priest chosen by lot to enter the sanctuary and burn incense within its sacred space. Since no one else could enter the sanctuary at the time, the people joined in the ceremony by praying outside. While he is offering incense, Zechariah becomes frightened at the angel's appearance. In accord with the standard literary format for heavenly visitations, Zechariah's fear leads the angel to tell him not to be afraid, a typical Old Testament greeting in response to a heavenly visitation. After bidding Zechariah not to fear, the angel declares that his prayers have been heard and that he and Elizabeth will conceive a son, whom they are to name John. Zechariah objects to the angel's revelation, stating that he and his wife are too old for the fulfillment of such a promise.

Luke identifies the angel as Gabriel, who stands in God's presence. This heavenly messenger was sent to bring the news of the birth of John to Zechariah. In this narrative, Gabriel announces that Zechariah will become mute until the message had been fulfilled because he questioned, doubting the heavenly message sent from God.

The angel, speaking for God, declares that the child shall be named John. The name means, "Yahweh has shown favor." All will rejoice over the birth of John, who will be great in the eyes of God and who will live the nazirite vow of never drinking strong drink or allowing a razor to touch his hair. (Numbers 6:1–4). Those who take the nazirite vow, which may be taken for a designated period of time, are considered "holy to the Lord" (Numbers 6:8). In the First Book of Samuel (1:22), we read that Hannah offers her son as a perpetual nazirite. The Holy Spirit will work through John, and he will be responsible for the return of many to the Lord. John the Baptist is also considered the new Elijah, a prophet sent to prepare the way of the Lord.

Luke adds a human touch to the story, as he does throughout his gospel. He notes that the people became impatient that Zechariah was in the sanctuary for such a long period. Their impatience changes to amazement when Zechariah comes out of the sanctuary, unable to speak. This becomes a sign for the people that Zechariah had received a vision while in the sanctuary. After his time of service in the Temple is finished, Zechariah goes home to Elizabeth, who conceived a child.

1:26–38 Annunciation of the birth of Jesus

When Matthew presents his infancy narrative, he centers it on Joseph, the husband of Mary. Luke centers his infancy narrative on Mary, although he does mention Joseph at significant points as he tells the story.

In the sixth month of Elizabeth's pregnancy, the angel Gabriel, who previously visited Zechariah, now comes to Mary, who is betrothed to Joseph of the house of David. Because the true line of inheritance comes through the father of the child and not through the mother, it is significant that Luke names Joseph as belonging to the lineage of David. Jesus, as the Messiah, must claim the line of David as his family line to fulfill the Old Testament expectation. Although Luke describes the birth of Jesus as a virgin birth, Jesus, according to Jewish Law, can claim the rights of the line of Joseph, who adopted him. Through adoption, one becomes a total heir of the adopting father, including the right to claim his lineage. Joseph, by taking Mary into his home, is accepting her child as his own.

The angel Gabriel now greets Mary by the name "favored one," telling the reader of Mary's position in God's eyes. The angel announces to Mary that the Lord is dwelling within her. Just as Zechariah was troubled by the words of the angel, so also is Mary troubled. Where Zechariah showed fear, Mary shows wonderment at the presence of the angel. The angel reassures her that she has found favor with God. The heavenly messenger further reveals to Mary that she will give birth to a son who will be given the name Jesus. Like John the Baptist, he will be a great prophet, but even more, he will be the Son of God (the Most High). By telling Mary that Jesus will take the throne of David, the angel actually announced that Jesus would be the promised Messiah. This message about Jesus was developed post-resurrection in the early Church, as a result of a richer and revealed understanding of the person of Jesus. The people who lived around the time of Jesus' birth would never have understood such a message.

Mary follows the customary practice of those who receive a message from an angel by pointing out the impossibility of the outcome. In her case, she declares she is a virgin. In the Old Testament, the presence of the Lord sojourned with the Israelites in the desert in the form of a cloud that overshadowed the tent. (See Exodus 40:34.) The Holy Spirit overshadows Mary, and this presence of the Lord brings about the conception of Jesus, the Son of God. Just as Zechariah received a sign that left him unable to speak, Mary also receives a sign, the pregnancy of Elizabeth. God brought about the impossible for Elizabeth, who was sterile, and Mary, who was a virgin. Both received a life where no life previously existed. Mary shows herself worthy of her discipleship by placing herself immediately at the service of the Lord. She proclaims, "Behold, I am the handmaid of the Lord." Like Jesus, who declared during his agony in the garden "not my will but yours be done," so Mary declares, "May it be done to me according to your word." Mary and Jesus are one in opening themselves to God's will.

1:39–56 Mary visits Elizabeth

Mary's journey to Elizabeth would ordinarily have taken four days. Upon her arrival, the child in the womb of Elizabeth leaps, thus proclaiming the arrival of Jesus living in the womb of Mary. Just as John would later point the way to the coming of the Lord during his ministry, so now, in his mother's womb, he performs his mission. In the presence of Jesus, Elizabeth receives the Holy Spirit, and just as John acknowledges Jesus as greater than himself, Elizabeth declares to Mary, "Most blessed are you among women, and blessed is the fruit of your womb."

In an Old Testament narrative about David and the sacred ark of God, David sees one of his men struck dead when he tries to steady the ark while they are carrying it. David feared for his own life and said, "How can the ark of the Lord come to me?" (2 Samuel 6:9). Elizabeth uses similar words as Mary enters her home, although she does not express them out of fear as David did. Mary is the ark of the Lord (Jesus) in the New Testament, and Elizabeth expresses her faith and humility by asking why the mother of the Lord should visit her. Elizabeth praises Mary for placing her trust in the message of the Lord.

Mary responds to the words of Elizabeth with a canticle (song) that recalls the canticle of Hannah at the birth of her son Samuel. (See 1 Samuel 2:1–10.) Mary proclaims that her whole person has now become a hymn of praise to God because of the great gift bestowed on her, a gift that will lead all people to refer to her as blessed. She praises God, who throughout the ages has raised the lowly above those who are powerful in the world. God shares all riches with the hungry and leaves the rich empty. Mary ends by proclaiming that God remembered the covenant made to Abraham and his descendants in this great gift that she bears within her. Her canticle alludes to many Old Testament prophecies that look forward to the coming of the Messiah. Mary remained with Elizabeth for three months, until the birth of Elizabeth's child. Although Luke seems to have her returning home before Elizabeth gives birth to John, he is simply concluding the story of Mary's visit to Elizabeth before he moves on to the story of the birth of John.

1:57–80 The birth of John

Luke, having completed his presentation of the parallel stories about the annunciation of the births of John and Jesus, now begins his parallel stories about their births. Eight days after the birth of a Jewish male child, the relatives would gather to celebrate the circumcision of the child as a sign of the covenant between God and the people of Israel. At this time, the father would give a name to the child. The name chosen usually reflected a common family name. Elizabeth, most likely following the instructions of Zechariah who cannot speak, names the child John, despite the protests of relatives who want to give the child his father's name. When Zechariah writes that the child's name shall be John, his speech returns as a sign of the Lord's acceptance of this name. The amazement of the crowd expresses the people's belief that this child was certainly marked by God for some great mission in life.

Zechariah immediately begins to praise God with a canticle known to many today as the Benedictus, which is Latin for the first word of the canticle, "Blessed." The canticle of Zechariah was most likely a prayer of praise that developed within the worship of the early Church and that Luke puts on the lips of Zechariah in this infancy narrative. Like the canticle of Mary, it has many subtle references to Old Testament writings. The canticle of Zechariah praises God for the fulfillment of the promise made to David and proclaimed through the saints and prophets of old.

Through the birth of John, God has brought salvation to Israel, as was promised through the covenant made with Abraham. Zechariah proclaims that John is the prophet of the Most High and has the mission of preparing the way of the Lord by teaching and leading the people to repentance. The end of the canticle reminds the reader that everything happens according to the plan of God, who gives light and guidance. Although Luke has not yet spoken of the birth of Jesus, he neatly concludes his story about the birth of John by summarizing his growth into adulthood and his life in the wilderness, where he begins his ministry.

Review Questions

1. Who is Theophilus? Explain.
2. What was so special about the birth of John the Baptist?
3. What words from the infancy narrative are found in the "Hail Mary"?
4. Why is Mary's Canticle so significant? Zechariah's Canticle?

Closing Prayer (SEE PAGE 14)

Pray the closing prayer now or after *lectio divina*.

Lectio Divina (SEE PAGE 7)

Relax your body and maintain a posture of prayer (back straight, eyes shut, feet flat on the floor). This exercise can take as long as you want, but in the context of this Bible study, 10 to 20 minutes should be sufficient.

The meditations that follow are provided only to help group participants use this prayer form, but note that *lectio* is intended to bring one to a place of prayerful contemplation where the Word of God speaks to the hearer from his or her heart. (See page 7 for further instruction.)

Luke gathers his sources (1:1–4)

Luke addresses his gospel to Theophilus, which means "Beloved of God." In presenting his message in an orderly fashion, Luke is helping us gain insight into God's astounding love for us. This love is made manifest in the life and message of Jesus Christ, the visible image of the invisible God. In Luke's Gospel, the "Beloved of God" learn how to become great lovers of God.

✠ *What can I learn from this passage?*

Annunciation of the birth of John the Baptist (1:5–25)

The prayers of Elizabeth and Zechariah led to the birth of John the Baptist. Both of John's parents were prayerful people. We do not know how much their prayers influenced the life of John the Baptist, but we can presume that Elizabeth and Zechariah continued to pray for John and his mission throughout their lives. The prayers of parents and friends often influence the lives of those we love in unseen ways.

✠ *What can I learn from this passage?*

Annunciation of the birth of Jesus (1:26–38)

Mary does not fully understand the message of the angel, but she willingly declares, "Behold, I am the handmaid of the Lord. May it be done to me according to your word." She becomes an example for all of us who make commitments to God, whether as a married person, a single person, an ordained priest, a religious, or a dedicated Christian. Together with Mary, we declare, "May it be done to me according to your word," and with Mary's help, we can remain faithful to our commitments, no matter how difficult they may become.

✠ *What can I learn from this passage?*

Mary visits Elizabeth (1:39–56)

When Mary visited Elizabeth, Elizabeth praised her for believing that what the Lord had told her would be fulfilled. Mary took no credit for her belief or for her great gift of being chosen as the Mother of Jesus. Instead, she proclaimed the greatness of the Lord. She recognized that God "has looked upon his handmaid's lowliness." Mary realized that it was all God's doing, not her own, proclaiming that "The Mighty One has done great things for me, and holy is his name."

✠ *What can I learn from this passage?*

The birth of John (1:57–80)

Luke tells us that Zechariah was "righteous in the eyes of God," a man of faith and prayer. His faith led him to believe that God would fulfill the promises God had made through the mouth of the prophets of old, but he never ceased to pray for this fulfillment. He lived righteously and prayed with faith. This Scripture passage invites us to become people of strong faith who pray as though everything in life depends on God and to act as though everything depends on us. God is our companion and guide.

✠ *What can I learn from this passage?*

PART 2: INDIVIDUAL STUDY

This lesson does not have an individual-study section.

LESSON 2

Preparation for Jesus' Public Ministry

LUKE 2:1—4:13

She wrapped him in swaddling clothes and laid him in a manger, because there was no room for them in the inn (2:7).

Opening Prayer (SEE PAGE 14)

Context

Part 1: Luke 2:1–52 Luke tells of the events surrounding the birth of Jesus, which include the journey of Mary and Joseph to Bethlehem, the homage paid to Jesus by the shepherds, the circumcision and presentation of Jesus in the Temple, and Mary's and Joseph's finding the twelve-year-old Jesus in the Temple after searching for him for three days.

Part 2: Luke 3:1—4:13 Luke describes the mission of John the Baptist, the events surrounding Jesus' baptism, the genealogy of Jesus, and Jesus' temptations in the desert.

PART 1: GROUP STUDY (LUKE 2:1–52)

Read aloud Luke 2:1–52.

2:1–20 The birth of Jesus

Earlier in his gospel, Luke placed the birth of John the Baptist at the center of the Jewish world by revealing Herod as the king of Judea. He now broadens his scope to include the whole known world when he speaks of the birth of Jesus. Jesus is born for all people, not just for the Jewish world. Luke states that a decree from Caesar Augustus ordered that a census of the "whole world should be enrolled."

When Luke writes his gospel some eighty or more years after the birth of Jesus, he does not seem to realize the difficulties presented in the historical names he uses. Herod, who is mentioned at the birth of John, died in 4 BC, while Quirinius, who is mentioned at the birth of Jesus, did not become governor of Syria until the year 6. A later census was taken when Jesus was about ten years old, and this would coincide with the time that Quirinius was governor of Syria. Luke, who is writing a religious message rather than a historical account of the birth of Jesus, was not concerned about this inaccuracy in his infancy narrative. The main purpose of the story is to show that Jesus' life touches the whole world.

Another purpose of citing the census in Luke's Gospel is the author's need to get Jesus from Nazareth to Bethlehem, which was the birthplace accepted by members of the early Church. In the Gospel of Matthew, Mary and Joseph reside in Bethlehem at the time of the birth of Jesus; only later do they go to Nazareth. Luke has the family of Jesus going from Nazareth to Bethlehem for the birth. Bethlehem is the town of David, from whose line the Messiah would come. Both gospels agree that Jesus is born in Bethlehem.

Luke mentions that Mary is engaged to Joseph, perhaps to further emphasize that a marriage had not yet taken place and that the birth was truly a virgin birth. Jesus is born and placed in a manger. The manger tells us that Jesus lives among the poor. Just as some of the Israelites would reject him throughout his life, they now reject him by refusing him lodging at the time of his birth. Mary gives birth to Jesus, who is called the "firstborn." The title does not mean Mary had other children. According to Jewish Law (Deuteronomy 21:15–17), the firstborn referred to the oldest male child who inherited all the gifts and traditions of the family. This was the position of privilege in the family. The title makes no statement concerning any future children or lack of children on the part of Mary and Joseph.

Just as Zechariah and Mary had received heavenly visitations from the angels of God, shepherds tending their sheep in a field now receive a similar visitation. Because they worked on the Sabbath and grazed their sheep on foreign land, the shepherds were considered outcasts by many of the Jews of Jesus' day. Luke has these outcasts become the heralds of Jesus' birth. The reaction of the shepherds to the heavenly visitation of an angel is described in the usual form used by scriptural authors in reporting such events. They react with fear, and the angel must calm their fear. The angel proclaims the joyful news that a savior, who is the Messiah and Lord, is born in Bethlehem. The sign given to the shepherds is the condition of lowliness in which Jesus is born, wrapped in bands of cloth and placed in a manger. The event is so great that all of the heavenly hosts join in the praise of God and proclaim that those who find favor with God will experience peace. This peace is a harmony and contentment that comes to those who know they are living in God's presence.

The shepherds, as symbols of the outcasts and sinners whom Jesus will meet during his life, respond as quickly as Mary did when she rushed to visit Elizabeth. They go to Bethlehem "with haste" and find Mary, Joseph, and Baby Jesus. When they see the Holy Family in this situation, they understand the message of the angel. The shepherds spread the word to others, who are equally astonished at their message. Luke tells us that Mary ponders all that is happening and concludes with the shepherds returning to the fields, praising God for all they have heard and seen.

2:21–40 The Presentation

On the eighth day, in accordance with Jewish Law, the Child is circumcised and given the name Jesus. In the Gospel of Matthew, the name, which means "God saves," is strongly emphasized. Luke, however, simply mentions that the name Jesus is given to the Child as the angel had directed before his conception. Luke confuses the story of the Presentation of Jesus with another ceremony, the purification of Mary. The presentation took place on the eighth day after the birth of a child. The author quotes from the Book of Exodus (13:2, 12) where Moses passes on the word of the Lord exhorting that the firstborn belongs to the Lord. Although the firstborn son belonged to the Lord, he could be ransomed by making an offering (13:13).

The purification of Mary should have taken place forty days after the birth of the male child, not on the eighth day after the child's birth (Leviticus 12:1–8). According to the Law of Moses, a woman who gives birth to a male child is considered unclean and must not touch anything sacred or enter the sanctuary for forty days. At the end of the forty days, she must present an offering to the priest, who will make an offering to the Lord for her, and she shall then be declared clean. The usual offering would be a lamb and a dove, but a poor person could offer two doves in place of the usual offering. Mary and Joseph make the offering of the poor. Luke portrays this offering as the ransom paid to the Lord for Jesus. In the First Book of Samuel (1:28), Samuel's mother, Hannah, does not ransom her child but leaves him in the Temple to serve the Lord.

Simeon, a prophet who lived in Jerusalem, recites the third canticle found in the infancy narrative. He has received the revelation by the inspiration of the Holy Spirit that he would not die before he saw the Messiah. The Spirit leads him to the Temple when Mary and Joseph come with Jesus. Commentators refer to Luke's Gospel as the Gospel of the Holy Spirit due to passages such as this where the activity of the Holy Spirit guides the people. When Simeon sees the child, he prays that God may now let him die. He does not name Jesus, but he declares that he has now witnessed the salvation God has prepared for the people. Simeon proclaims that the child has come as "a light for revelation to the Gentiles, and glory for your people Israel." He further prophesies that Jesus will be responsible for the fall and rise of many in Israel, perhaps referring to the religious leaders who will reject Jesus and the disciples who will accept him. He prophesies to Mary that she will suffer along with Jesus, as she does by witnessing his struggles in ministry and his passion and death.

Anna, an elderly prophetess who has spent most of her life in the

Temple fasting and praying, also gives witness to the ministry of Jesus. Throughout this gospel, Luke will emphasize the special role of women in the life of Jesus. Anna is just one of many women who recognizes Jesus and his mission. She thanks God for Jesus and becomes an evangelist for those who were awaiting the redemption of Jerusalem by faith in God.

The passage ends with Mary and Joseph's returning home with Jesus, who grows in the normal manner, physically and spiritually, and who (Luke tells us) is "filled with wisdom; and the favor of God was upon him."

2:41–52 The boy Jesus in the Temple

Many of the Jews who lived outside Jerusalem returned each year to the holy city for the major feast of Israel, Passover. Mary and Joseph, who were accustomed to going to Jerusalem for the feast, take Jesus with them when he reaches the age of twelve. On their way home, Mary and Joseph discover that Jesus is missing, and they return to Jerusalem in search of him. They find him "after three days," alluding to the resurrection of Jesus that will occur three days after his death.

Jesus seems surprised that his parents should be looking for him. He apparently is experiencing the early impulses of his mission, and he implies that his parents should have realized where he was, namely, in the house of God. The ease with which Jesus refers to God as his Father is significant, but it is beyond the grasp of Mary and Joseph. Although Jesus will remain obedient to his parents, he is here showing a greater call to follow the will of God the Father. Mary stores these mysteries in her mind. The Scriptures tell us that Mary "kept all these things in her heart." Jesus returns home with Mary and Joseph and lives in obedience to them, growing in wisdom, age, and grace according to Luke.

Review Questions

1. Name some parallels between the birth of John the Baptist and the birth of Jesus.
2. What hints in the infancy narrative lead us to believe the story was written after the resurrection of Jesus?
3. What lessons do we learn from the story of Jesus who remained for three days in the Temple at the age of twelve?

Closing Prayer (SEE PAGE 14)

Pray the closing prayer now or after *lectio divina*.

Lectio Divina (SEE PAGE 7)

Relax your body and maintain a posture of prayer (back straight, eyes shut, feet flat on the floor). This exercise can take as long as you want, but in the context of this Bible study, 10 to 20 minutes should be sufficient.

The meditations that follow are provided only to help group participants use this prayer form, but note that *lectio* is intended to bring one to a place of prayerful contemplation where the Word of God speaks to the hearer from his or her heart. (See page 7 for further instruction.)

The birth of Jesus (2:1–20)

Jesus comes for all people. The shepherds, considered sinners in the eyes of the people of Jesus' day, are the first to receive the good news of the birth of Jesus. The outcasts are suddenly the rewarded ones. Throughout the gospel, we will learn that sinners are a priority in Jesus' mission. He said he came to call sinners, not the just. This is good news for all of us.

✠ *What can I learn from this passage?*

The Presentation (2:21–40)

When parents celebrate the baptism of their child, a joyful experience could turn into a chilling experience if someone were to predict that the child would be accepted by some but rejected and contradicted by many others. After receiving Simeon's dire message, Jesus' parents return home to Nazareth, undeterred in their commitment to God.

✠ *What can I learn from this passage?*

The boy Jesus in the Temple (2:41–52)

Pondering, as Mary often did, is a part of commitment. When we commit ourselves to the Lord, we do not receive a clear map of our life ahead. Rather, true commitment requires deep trust and is often accompanied by confusion and even periods of doubt. Like Mary, we might wonder where God is leading us. We can follow her example by complete surrender to God's will.

✠ *What can I learn from this passage?*

PART 2: INDIVIDUAL STUDY (LUKE 3:1—4:13)

Day 1: The Preaching of John the Baptist (3:1–20)

In the third section of Luke's Gospel, the author speaks of Jesus' preparation for his ministry by introducing the reader to John the Baptist and his mission. This is followed by Jesus' preparation for his baptism and temptations in the desert. Through the genealogy of Jesus, the author shows that Jesus' ancestry can be traced back to Adam, since he depicts Jesus as a universal savior.

Continuing to use his framework of a universal salvation during the ministry of Jesus, Luke places the ministry of John within the context of the history of the Roman world. The Word of God comes to John in the desert in the "fifteenth year of the reign of Emperor Tiberius," which places the date somewhere between the years 27 and 29. After naming the ruler of the entire Roman Empire, Luke narrows the scene to the Roman rulers in and around Palestine.

After the death of Herod the Great in 4 BC, the land of Palestine was divided among his sons. One son, Archelaus, ruled so badly that his portion of the lands, mainly those of Judea, were turned over to a Roman procurator. At the time of John's preaching in the desert, the procurator was Pontius Pilate. Other lands around Palestine were ruled by Herod, Philip, and Lysanias.

Luke names two high priests for this period, but the actual high priest was Caiaphas. Caiaphas's father-in-law, Annas, held the position until the year 15, when he turned it over to his daughter's husband. Annas, however, kept such control over the office that many considered him an acting high priest. For this reason Luke names the two of them as high priests.

When Luke tells us that the Word of God came to John, he again declares that John is the son of Zechariah, thus linking this part of the story with the infancy narrative. Luke follows Mark in much of his presentation about John. The Baptist calls the people to a baptism that demands a change of heart. Luke identifies John as the one foretold by Isaiah who will prepare the way of the Lord. Luke adds two more verses to those found in the parallel passages in Mark and Matthew. He states that "all flesh shall see the salvation of God," thus adding a reference to a central message of his gospel, namely, that Jesus came for the salvation of all people (Isaiah 40:5).

John addresses his audience as a "brood of vipers," a dreadful and insulting accusation in John's era. He challenges them to produce good fruit, performing good works as a sign of their repentance. They should not make the false assumption that they are favored by God simply because they are descendants of Abraham. By telling them that God can raise up children to Abraham from the abundance of stones in the desert, he is teaching them that anyone can be a child of Abraham, but the real challenge is to live in the spirit of Abraham. The time of reckoning is near for "the ax lies at the root of the trees," and the people must show some signs that they have reformed their lives.

John's words begin to influence many of his listeners who now ask what they should do. His first response to the crowd is to share what they have, whether clothing or food. His words are so powerful that even tax collectors and soldiers ask what they should do. John does not tell them to abandon their trade, but he tells tax collectors to be fair in collecting taxes; soldiers that they should avoid extortion, false accusations, and become satisfied with their wages. Luke alone mentions these groups, thus showing the importance of outcasts in his gospel. It is significant that Luke does not reject the tax collectors and soldiers whom the Jewish people generally hated. Rather, he portrays John as someone who allowed them to remain in their trade as long as they were fair. This is the good fruit they must produce as a sign of their repentance.

John declares that one mightier than he will come who will baptize them not only with water, but with the Holy Spirit and fire. The allusion is to show the power of the Spirit and the cleansing power of fire. Yet some see these words as pointing to the day of Pentecost when the Holy Spirit comes upon the disciples in the form of tongues of fire. John explains that the one who is to come is so far superior to him that he is not even worthy to perform the act of a lowly servant, namely, to loosen the thongs of Jesus' sandals. The time of judgment has arrived when God will gather the good (wheat) into the barn and burn the evil ones (chaff) with unquenchable fire. The discourse of John in this gospel is completed with the notion that John preached the good news to the people.

This section ends with John's imprisonment by Herod the tetrarch because John accused Herod of an improper marriage to Herodias, his brother's wife, and rebuked him for his other crimes.

Lectio Divina

Spend 8 to 10 minutes in silent contemplation of the following passage:

John is preparing the people for the coming of Christ by calling those who have been blessed with gifts to share them with others and those who have worked to perform their tasks well. John does not tell tax collectors and soldiers to quit their work, but he admonishes them to perform their tasks justly and well. John's words sound very much like the directions given by Jesus in the gospels. In doing this, John is preparing the way of the Lord.

✠ *What can I learn from this passage?*

Day 2: God's Beloved Son (3:21–38)

Luke does not describe the baptism of Jesus but shows Jesus at prayer after he was baptized. In the midst of this prayer, the Holy Spirit descends upon Jesus, and a voice from heaven proclaims Jesus as "the beloved Son" of the Father. In this gospel, Jesus is portrayed as a man of prayer, especially before important events. Jesus prays: before he chooses the Twelve (6:12); when he prays in solitude with his disciples (9:18); at the time of the transfiguration (9:28); before he teaches his disciples to pray (11:1); at the Last Supper when he declares that he has prayed for Peter (22:32); during his agony in the garden (22:41); and on the cross (23:46). The gospel writer does not indicate whether anyone besides Jesus saw the descent of the Holy Spirit and heard the voice from heaven.

Matthew puts the genealogy of Jesus at the beginning of his gospel. Luke, however, places it after Jesus' baptism, perhaps to show the importance of Jesus' commitment to his mission. The genealogies found in Matthew and Luke differ from each other, an indication that the gospels are primarily religious books with a message and not history books in a strict sense.

Matthew shows that Jesus is a true Israelite, and he traces his family tree back to Abraham, the father of the Israelite nation.

Luke, however, wishes to show that Jesus came for all people, so he traces the family line of Jesus back to Adam, the father of all people and then to God, the creator of all. The genealogies do not agree with each other at all points, showing that each writer chose the names in the genealogy to fit the purpose of their narratives. Luke does not end with Adam, but adds that Adam is a son of God, perhaps to emphasize Jesus' divine sonship. Both genealogies link the line of Jesus with that of his foster-father, Joseph. In accepting Jesus as his own, Joseph gave him the right to the line of Abraham and David.

Matthew begins his genealogy moving down the line from Abraham to Jesus, whereas Luke begins with Jesus and moves up the line to Adam and then to God. He mentions that Jesus was about thirty years of age when he began his ministry. When he identifies Jesus as the son of Joseph, he adds the phrase "as was thought," thereby remaining faithful to his message that Jesus was of a virgin birth. Since Luke presents Jesus as the prophet in his narrative, he names Nathan the prophet as the son of David instead of Solomon, thus emphasizing Jesus' role as a prophet.

Lectio Divina

Spend 8 to 10 minutes in silent contemplation of the following passage:

> Just as the heavens were opened and the Holy Spirit descended upon Jesus in his prayer after his baptism by John, so the heavens open at every baptism, joining all the baptized to Jesus as brothers and sisters. Just as parents can say to their child, "Make me proud of you," so God can say to each of us, "Make me proud of you!"

✠ *What can I learn from this passage?*

Day 3: Temptations in the Desert (4:1–13)

Luke uses the same source ("the sayings of Jesus") as Matthew does for his story of the temptations of Jesus in the desert, although he reverses the order of the second and third temptations. Luke states that the Spirit leads Jesus into the desert for forty days to be tempted by the devil, as though the temptations were the reason for Jesus' sojourn in the desert. The forty days are reminiscent of the forty years' sojourn of the Israelites in the desert after their escape from Egypt. Where the Israelites failed, Jesus will succeed.

During the time of Jesus, the desert was considered the abode of demons, so it would be the logical place for the devil to tempt Jesus. At the end of Jesus' forty days of fasting, Luke mentions that Jesus is hungry. The devil is aware that the voice from heaven at Jesus' baptism by John proclaimed, "You are my beloved Son" (3:22), so he uses the sonship of Jesus as the challenge in his temptations. He will begin with the words, "If you are the Son of God."

Taking advantage of Jesus' identity and of his hunger, he challenges Jesus to show that he is the Son of God by tempting him to change the stones in the desert to bread. Jesus responds with a quote from the Book of Deuteronomy (8:3), declaring that a person does not live on bread alone.

The devil then showed Jesus all the kingdoms of the world, remarking that they all belong to him, and then offering them to Jesus if he were to bow down and worship the evil one. As the Son of God, Jesus will spiritually rule all the kingdoms of the world in his glory, but he will reach this eternal glory through his passion, death, and resurrection. Jesus has no desire for worldly glory, fame, or wealth. He quotes from the Book of Deuteronomy (6:13) by declaring that all people are called to worship and serve the Lord alone.

The devil then takes Jesus to the parapet of the Temple and challenges him as the Son of God to throw himself off. The devil quotes from Psalm 91:11–12, reminding Jesus that the Scriptures declare that the angels will guard him lest he even dash his foot against a stone. Jesus responds that the Scriptures also say that a person should not put the Lord, your God, to the test (Deuteronomy 6:16). In Jesus' day, a rabbi would debate with another rabbi by quoting a text from Scripture to prove his point. The other rabbi would respond by quoting from another part of the Scriptures to refute him. In this last temptation, the devil quotes from Scripture, and Jesus refutes him by quoting from another part of the Scripture, which has more force. With this last temptation, the devil departs, but Luke adds the words "for a time," thus showing that Jesus and the devil will have a later confrontation in the gospel.

Lectio Divina

Spend 8 to 10 minutes in silent contemplation of the following passage:

> In many ways, we experience the same temptations endured by Jesus. We will be tempted to abandon God for worldly desires or to make material goods and prestige something we worship more than God. Like Jesus, we have our calling and must respond to it, expecting worldly temptations, struggles, disappointments, and confusion to be always a part of our life. Jesus calls us to remain faithful as he did.

✠ *What can I learn from this passage?*

Review Questions

1. What is the mission and message of John the Baptist?
2. Why is it significant that John baptized Jesus?
3. How does Luke's genealogy differ from the one found in Matthew's Gospel?
4. How do the temptations of Jesus compare with our own temptations?

Jesus' Ministry in Galilee

LUKE 4:14—6:26

"The Spirit of the Lord is upon me, because he has anointed me to bring glad tidings to the poor" (4:18).

Opening Prayer (SEE PAGE 14)

Context

Part 1: Luke 4:14—5:11 The author tells of Jesus' ministry in Galilee, which begins with his rejection by the people of his own hometown, and continues with a series of miracles, including casting a demon out of a man and the healing of Peter's mother-in-law. Jesus chooses three of his disciples through the miracle of catching a large number of fish.

Part 2: Luke 5:12—6:26 In this section, Luke presents five conflict stories, chooses the Twelve Apostles, and preaches the Beatitudes.

PART 1: GROUP STUDY (LUKE 4:14—5:11)

Read aloud Luke 4:14—5:11.

4:14–30 The beginning of Jesus' mission in Galilee

Luke begins the forth division of his narrative, which speaks of Jesus' ministry in Galilee. Now that Jesus has finished the preparation for his ministry and has successfully overcome the temptations of the devil, he moves to Galilee where he will perform his miracles and teach a major portion of his message. The mission in Galilee will allow Luke to stress Jesus' universal mission to all people.

The Spirit leads Jesus back to Galilee, just as he was led into the desert. Jesus came from Galilee to be baptized by John, and now he returns to begin his public ministry. Although Luke has said nothing yet about Jesus' miraculous deeds or his preaching, he portrays Jesus' popularity as growing among the people. News about Jesus was spreading rapidly throughout the whole region, a theme frequently presented in this gospel. Jesus is portrayed as a teacher early in Luke's Gospel, receiving praise from all the people when he teaches in their synagogues. The plural use of the word *synagogues* shows Jesus as a type of itinerant preacher who travels from synagogue to synagogue.

Luke tells us that Jesus returned to his hometown early in his ministry, while Matthew and Mark speak of Jesus in Nazareth a bit later. He tells us that Jesus went to the synagogue on the Sabbath, "according to his custom." Jesus, the good Jew, was one who felt the need to pray with his community on every Sabbath. Here we see him taking the scroll and reading from the Book of Isaiah (61:1–2), a passage that stresses the role of the Spirit in the life of the chosen one. Jesus applies this passage to himself, the one upon whom the Spirit of the Lord comes and anoints with the mission of bringing the Good News to the poor, proclaiming liberty to captives, giving sight to the blind, bringing freedom to the oppressed, and declaring a year acceptable to the Lord. In the Old Testament, prophets of God were considered the anointed ones. Jesus is proclaiming that he is anointed by God for his mission as a prophet. By proclaiming that "this

Scripture passage is fulfilled in your hearing, he is proclaiming that he is the fulfillment of the Old Testament promises.

The immediate response of the people to Jesus' words is favorable, but soon they begin to bicker and question. Although the crowd at first likes what they hear, they remember that he is the son of Joseph, as ordinary as they are. Jesus anticipates this reaction and, recognizing human nature, declares that a prophet is not acceptable in his own native place. Because they knew him as he grew up in their midst, they could not accept that he was as exceptional as people said he was. Jesus refers to the proverb, "Physician, cure yourself," acknowledging their desire for him to perform signs and wonders in his native place to ease their doubts. He will hear a similar remark thrust at him on the cross when someone says that he saved others, so let him save himself if he is the Messiah (Luke 23:35).

Jesus further antagonizes his listeners when he alludes to the Jewish prophets Elijah and Elisha, who brought the gifts of God to people other than the Israelites because the Chosen People refused to accept them. He reminds his listeners of the widow of Zeraphath who offered the last of her flour and oil to the prophet Elijah, forgetting her own need and that of her son. Because of her respect for the prophet, she miraculously received from God enough for herself and her family for a long period, and in time, her son died and was raised by Elijah (1 Kings 17:1–24). Jesus also refers to the healing of a foreign Syrian soldier named Naaman who was a leper and who was cured of his leprosy by following the direction of Elisha the prophet (2 Kings 5:1–14).

The insulted and enraged people rise up and drive Jesus from the town, leading him to the brow of a hill with the intention of hurling him over it, but Jesus passes through their midst and leaves them. His hour had not yet come.

4:31–44 Jesus casts out demons

Luke follows Mark closely by narrating a typical day in the life of Jesus. On a Sabbath day, Jesus travels to Capernaum in Galilee, amazing the crowds with his teachings in the synagogue and his confrontation with an unclean spirit. A demon cries out to Jesus through the mouth of a possessed man, asking Christ if he intends to destroy him. In the Gospel of Luke, as in the Gospel of Mark, Jesus orders the unclean spirit to be silent when he identifies Jesus as the "Holy One of God." In Jesus' era, to correctly identify someone was to have control over that person. Although Luke is using this section from Mark, he seems to be using this passage to show Jesus' power over unclean spirits. In a typical last effort of power, the demon harmlessly casts the man down and comes out of him. The people viewed this power over unclean spirits as a form of teaching with authority. Yet Jesus teaches with both words and deeds.

Although Jesus has not yet chosen his disciples in Luke's Gospel, the author of the gospel tells of Jesus going to the home of Simon. Since Mark had previously named Simon and Andrew as two of the disciples chosen before this event, Mark's Gospel identifies the house as that of Simon and Andrew. Simon's mother-in-law was suffering from a high fever, which Jesus treats in the same manner as demon possession. Luke tells us that they interceded for her, as though they were praying. Jesus not only cures her but rebukes the fever as though he were rebuking demons, and the fever leaves her. Just as the disciples of Jesus must follow his example of service, Simon's mother-in-law takes the role of a disciple, gets up, and waits on Jesus and his companions.

Jesus ends the day curing the sick by laying hands on them. The people of Jesus' day saw sickness as a sign of sin or some evil possession. They believed that by curing the sick, Jesus was casting out demons. The demons shout out the true identity of Jesus as the Son of God, and Luke again follows Mark's use of the "messianic secret" as Jesus orders the demons to keep silent. Mark writes that Jesus silenced the demons because they knew him, whereas Luke adds that it was because they knew he was the Messiah. If the people began to proclaim Jesus as the Messiah (Christ in Greek), his mission would have been jeopardized, since many believed the Messiah would be a warrior messiah who would free Israel from Roman rule. The Roman authorities would be quick to squelch anyone whom the people followed as a messiah, but Jesus' mission was one of spiritual salvation for all people, not a political salvation.

The next morning, Jesus goes off to a deserted place and, in contrast to the people of Nazareth who rejected him, these crowds attempt to keep Jesus with them. In Mark's Gospel, Simon and the other disciples go looking for Jesus, but in Luke the crowds went looking for him. Jesus tells them that his mission is to announce the Good News of the kingdom of God to other towns.

5:1–11 *The call of Jesus' first disciples*

The crowd following Jesus becomes so immense that the people are now "pressing in on" him to listen to the word of God. Luke alone refers to the Sea of Galilee as the Lake of Gennesaret, due most likely to the fact that the area of Gennesaret lies at the northwest corner of the sea. To avoid being pushed into the sea by the crowd, Jesus climbs into Simon's boat and preaches to the people from there.

As a sign of his authority, Jesus preaches from a sitting position, a commonly accepted position for one in authority. After preaching, Jesus tells Simon to sail out into deeper water and lower his nets. Although it was a most unlikely hour for fishing, Simon, who had been fishing all night with no results, obediently drops his nets into the water. He pulls in so many fish that his nets were breaking from the overwhelming catch. He signaled to another boat for help, and the catch of fish filled both boats so that they were nearly sinking. When Simon (now Simon Peter) sees the miraculous number of fish, he recognizes for the first time the greatness of Jesus and falls to his knees, begging Jesus to leave him because he is a sinful man.

Luke uses this occasion for Jesus to call his first disciples, namely, Peter, James, and John. Jesus admonishes them not to be afraid, since they will now be catching people instead of fish. The three disciples leave everything to become followers of Jesus. In Mark's Gospel, Peter, Andrew, James, and John leave their boats, nets, and families to follow Jesus at the beginning of Jesus' ministry before they witness the healing power of Jesus. At this point in Luke's Gospel, the disciples have witnessed the healing power of Jesus, his power over demons, and the miraculous catch of fish, which are strong motives for leaving all to follow Jesus.

Review Questions

1. How does Jesus' mission in Galilee begin? Explain.

2. What is the significance of the voice from heaven that declares Jesus is a "beloved Son"? (Luke 3:22)

3. What is the role of the Holy Spirit in the life of Jesus?

Closing Prayer (SEE PAGE 14)

Pray the closing prayer now or after *lectio divina*.

Lectio Divina (SEE PAGE 7)

Relax your body and maintain a posture of prayer (back straight, eyes shut, feet flat on the floor). This exercise can take as long as you want, but in the context of this Bible study, 10 to 20 minutes should be sufficient.

The meditations that follow are provided only to help group participants use this prayer form, but note that *lectio* is intended to bring one to a place of prayerful contemplation where the Word of God speaks to the hearer from his or her heart. (See page 7 for further instruction.)

The beginning of Jesus' mission in Galilee (4:14–30)

Recognizing the activity of the Spirit in our midst demands a deep faith, one that accepts a belief that the Holy Spirit can use us to share the message of Jesus through our words and actions. The Spirit can also use others who may seem insignificant to us or too ordinary to be someone specially sent by God for us. Like the people of Nazareth, we may refuse to listen to these prophets because we "know them" and expect so little from them. We can pray to recognize the prophets in our lives.

✠ *What can I learn from this passage?*

Jesus' healing power (4:31–44)

After performing a number of healings for the people, Jesus arose early in the morning to escape the crowd for a period of prayer. His excited disciples wanted him to come back and enjoy the adulation of the people, but Jesus, in his prayer, was able to recognize that he must continue on his journey to spread his message to other towns and villages. Just as periods of prayer

---

helped Jesus recognize the direction of his ministry in life, so it helped all other followers of Christ to do the same—laity, religious, and so forth.

✠ *What can I learn from this passage?*

The call of Jesus' first disciples (5:1–11)

The incident of the miraculous catch of fish illustrates that the Church did not begin with highly educated personnel but with simple fishermen whose work left little time for learning. If Jesus placed his trust in the intelligent leaders of his day, we may have felt that the Church grew through their ingenuity. Instead, by choosing uneducated fishermen as his first disciples, Jesus was showing that the birth and growth of the Church would truly be miraculous. In our world today, many of Jesus' followers may be highly educated, but they realize they are striving to catch the hearts of people, and this cannot be done by intellect alone, but with the grace of God.

✠ *What can I learn from this passage?*

PART 2: INDIVIDUAL STUDY (LUKE 5:12—6:26)

Day 1: The Cleansing of a Man With Leprosy (5:12–16)

Although Luke continues to follow the Gospel of Mark closely, the messages contained in some of the stories take on a different meaning. Luke shows Jesus' special concern for the downtrodden, the outcast, and the lowly of Jewish society. A man with leprosy, an outcast of society, seeks a cure from Jesus. He expresses his faith in Jesus by addressing him with the title of faith, calling him "Lord," and stating his belief that Jesus can cure him if he chooses. Jesus, using the man's words, touches him and responds that he wills to do so, and he cures him. Jesus, true to the demands of Jewish Law, directs the man to show himself to the priest and to make the proper offering in accordance with the Law of Moses (Leviticus 14:1–32). The news about Jesus spreads as he continues to teach and cure the people, and large crowds listened to his words. Luke again stresses the prayerfulness of Jesus when he emphasizes that Christ would depart to deserted places to pray.

Lectio Divina

Spend 8 to 10 minutes in silent contemplation of the following passage:

> The man with leprosy places God's will above all else by declaring, "Lord, if you wish, you can make me clean." Many people live with sickness, disease, disabilities, pain, and the recognition that death is near, yet still they pray. To be able to say at times such as this, "Not my will, but yours be done," is difficult, but God has a better insight into our needs than we do.

✠ *What can I learn from this passage?*

Day 2: Jesus Heals a Paralyzed Man (5:17–26)

Luke begins the first of five conflict stories involving Jesus and the religious leaders with the passage about forgiving and healing a man who was paralyzed. This healing story of the paralyzed man comes from the Gospel of Mark. Luke indicates that the healing power of the Lord was with Jesus when the friends of the paralyzed man were unable to get to Christ because of the large crowd. Thus they lower him through the roof of the place where Jesus is preaching. In Mark's Gospel, the men open up the roof, referencing the manner in which the roofs of houses in Palestine were constructed with straw and clay. Luke, who is addressing a Gentile audience, is familiar with other areas of the Roman world that had roofs made of tile. In contrast, we read that the paralyzed man is lowered through tiles, though the story was told differently by Mark.

When Jesus witnesses the faith of the men and the paralyzed man, he forgives the paralyzed man's sins. The Pharisees and scribes who are present know that the power of forgiving sin belongs to God alone, and they accuse Jesus of blasphemy. Aware that the people believe that sickness is a sign of all evil power controlling a person, Jesus asks the religious leaders what they consider easier, to forgive sins or to heal. Jesus shows that he has the power to forgive sins by commanding the paralyzed man to rise, pick up his mat, and go home. As the paralyzed man went home praising God, the crowds were awestruck.

Lectio Divina

Spend 8 to 10 minutes in silent contemplation of the following passage:

After Jesus heals the paralyzed man of his sinfulness, he heals his body as well. He tells him to pick up his mat and walk, and the paralyzed man goes home, praising God. His life had changed. Not only could he walk, he was now walking with the Lord and experienced a complete conversion, a true miracle of reconciliation.

✠ *What can I learn from this passage?*

Day 3: Conflicts Concerning Dining (5:27–39)

Jesus' second and third conflict stories occur at a meal. The second conflict story concerns Jesus' eating and drinking with those the Pharisees considered to be sinners. The Pharisees believed that tax collectors, who acted on behalf of Rome and sometimes cheated the people of their own nation, were obviously sinners. They are scandalized when Jesus calls Levi from his tax-collecting post to become one of his disciples. They become further outraged when Jesus goes to the house of Levi, who as a true disciple, has left everything to follow Jesus. At the house, Jesus dines with tax collectors and others. To dine with a person during Jesus' era was to identify in some way with that person's manner of life. The Pharisees and scribes do not protest directly to Jesus, but they complain to his disciples, asking why Jesus would dare to eat with tax collectors and sinners.

This second conflict story contains a pronouncement by Jesus. In the gospels, when Jesus adds a short statement or lesson at the end of a story or an event, it is known as a pronouncement story. At the end of this passage, Jesus makes a pronouncement about his mission to help those in need of healing. Just as sick people need a physician, sinners need Jesus. Jesus reverses the idea that eating with sinners indicates Jesus' acceptance of their manner of life; instead he exhorts that they are dining with him and accepting Jesus' manner of life.

The third conflict story occurs in the same place as the second and concerns the practice of fasting. Whereas the Pharisees and the disciples of John fast, the disciples of Jesus did not. In the Old Testament, the coming of the Messiah was occasionally referred to as a type of wedding feast. Jesus, the Messiah, is the bridegroom, and as long as he is in the world, there is no reason to fast. It is a time for rejoicing. Jesus looks toward the time of his death, when the bridegroom will no longer be with them; then they must fast. The evangelist could be teaching the members of the early community about the true motive behind their fasting. They do not fast out of sorrow, but rather as a response to the privilege of sharing in the reign of God and all it demands.

Jesus further clarifies his message of a change in attitude with the image of a new patch sewn on an old cloth. The new patch will not match the old and will tear at the first washing. In the same way, new wine poured into old wineskins will cause the old skins to burst and the wine will be lost. Jesus is warning his listeners that a person who tries to make the new fit the old will lose both. The reasons for dieting as prescribed in the Law of Moses cease to be necessary, particularly for Gentile communities, but fasting is still vital for followers of Jesus. The images of the new patch and new wine presented by Jesus stress the difficulty humans often have of accepting change. Implied here is the idea that the new wine could be better than the old, but because the people have not acquired a taste for it, they will reject it.

Lectio Divina

Spend 8 to 10 minutes in silent contemplation of the following passage:

The eucharistic celebration welcomes sinners with the hope that the grace of God will touch our hearts and bring about a conversion. In the eucharistic celebration, Jesus welcomes saints and sinners to join him in the meal, and Jesus, the bridegroom, celebrates with us.

✠ *What can I learn from this passage?*

Day 4: The Question About the Sabbath (6:1–11)

The fourth and fifth conflict stories center on the Sabbath rest. The fourth one concerns the laws about work on the Sabbath. As Jesus and his disciples are going through a field of grain on the Sabbath, the disciples pull off the head of the grain, grind it in their hands, and eat it. According to the Pharisees, such an action is considered work, which is forbidden on the Sabbath. Jesus intervenes and recalls an incident in the Old Testament where David entered the Temple when his soldiers were hungry, took the holy bread reserved for the priests, and gave it to his army to eat. The priest at the time recognized that the need to feed hungry men came before the strict observance of the Law. Once Jesus makes his point concerning the proper attitude toward work on the Sabbath, he follows with a further pronouncement, referring to himself as the Son of Man and adding that he is the Lord of the Sabbath. Jesus occasionally uses the term Son of Man for himself in place of *I* when he is referring to himself in his humanity. In this passage, Luke uses it as equivalent to Lord. Jesus, the Son of Man, is Lord of the Sabbath.

The fifth and final conflict between Jesus and the scribes and Pharisees also takes place on a Sabbath. The gospel presents the story as though the scribes and Pharisees had set up a situation in which Jesus would condemn himself. They watch as Jesus encounters a man with a withered hand in the Temple. According to Jewish Law, one could save a life on the Sabbath but do little else. Jesus asks the leaders of the people if it is lawful on the Sabbath to do good or evil. If Jesus cures the man, he implies he will be performing a good act. If he refuses to cure him, he implies he is choosing to do evil. Jesus extends the law of the Sabbath to include the performance of all good actions, and he heals the man with the withered hand. The scribes and Pharisees, rebuffed in the five conflict stories, now ask one another what they can do about Jesus.

In correcting the attitudes of the religious leaders about the Sabbath, Jesus is also preparing a new community of disciples for the fulfillment of the Law. Jesus chooses Twelve Apostles, who will become the leaders of the new Israel, just as the twelve sons of Jacob represented the old Israel. Before he chooses the Twelve Apostles, a major event in the reign of God,

Jesus departs to a mountain and spends the night in prayer. The people of Israel viewed the image of a mountain as a place where God visited God's people, a place closer to God in heaven. Luke uses the term *apostle,* meaning "one who is sent," more often than the other synoptic gospels, thus implying that the Twelve will be sent out to share the message of Jesus.

Lectio Divina

Spend 8 to 10 minutes in silent contemplation of the following passage:

> The true Sabbath rest is intended for the good of developing one's relationship with God and neighbor. The Sabbath rest is given, not to limit a person's movements, recreation, or necessary work, but for the purpose of setting aside a reasonable amount of time for human beings to worship God.

✠ *What can I learn from this passage?*

Day 5: The Sermon on the Plain (6:12–26)

The Beatitudes are presented on the plain in Luke's Gospel, in direct contrast with the Sermon on the Mount described in the Gospel of Matthew. The gospel writer's presentation is a possible parallel to Moses' action of bringing the commandments down the mountain to the Israelites.

Luke mentions only four Beatitudes, and he speaks directly to his listeners by using the word *you.* Unlike Matthew, Luke does not speak of an attitude of mind but more of a condition that already exists. He speaks of the blessedness of the poor rather than the poor in spirit as found in the Gospel of Matthew. In Luke, we visualize Jesus saying blessed are the ones who are hungry, mourning, persecuted, or insulted because of him. Jesus refers to himself as the Son of Man in this passage. Those who are treated unjustly and shamefully for the sake of Jesus have a reason to rejoice, because those who endure such treatment will find an eternal reward awaiting them.

Luke follows an Old Testament practice of linking the woes with the blessings of God (Deuteronomy 27:14—28:6). The woes parallel the Beatitudes by presenting the punishment in store for those who are the opposite of the blessed ones. Woe to the rich, the full, the nonsorrowing, and those held in high esteem in the world. The woes are mentioned not because people have these gifts in their lives, but because they do not use them properly. They have already received their reward. Jesus reminds his listeners that their ancestors treated the prophets with scorn and shame while false prophets received undeserved praise.

Lectio Divina

Spend 8 to 10 minutes in silent contemplation of the following passage:

Those who choose to sacrifice their lives for Christ may appear to be poor, hungry, grieving, or rejected, but they are blessed in God's eyes. Those who strive to live a life of wealth, total fulfillment, pleasure, or fame at the cost of ignoring others have nothing in God's eyes. Their life is aimless and shallow, because in the end, they will have nothing. Those who live for Christ are the richest people in the world.

✠ *What can I learn from this passage?*

Review Questions

1. What is significant about Jesus' cure of the man with leprosy?
2. Why was it important for Jesus to heal the paralyzed man?
3. What message do we find in Jesus' eating and drinking with sinners?
4. What is Jesus condemning when he says "woe to you…"?

Jesus Teaches and Heals

LUKE 6:27—8:56

They are like children who sit in the marketplace and call to one another, "We played the flute for you, but you did not dance. We sang a dirge, but you did not weep" (7:32).

Opening Prayer (SEE PAGE 14)

Context

Part 1: Luke 6:27—7:35 Jesus teaches love of enemies, avoidance of judging others, the need to bear good fruit, and to build faith on a firm foundation. He heals a centurion's servant and raises a man from the dead for the sake of his mother. John the Baptist sends messengers to Jesus, questioning whether they should they look for another Messiah. Jesus points to his healing and preaching as proof that he is the one, and he praises John for his ministry.

Part 2: Luke 7:36—8:56 Jesus is anointed with expensive oil by a woman known to be a sinner, exhorting that the woman's love is great because she understands the value of forgiveness. Jesus also relates the parable of the sower, the parable of the lamp, calms the storm and heals a man possessed by many demons.

PART 1: GROUP STUDY (LUKE 6:27—7:35)

Read aloud Luke 6:27—7:35.

6:27–49 Living as a follower of Jesus

As with Matthew, Luke strings together a series of Jesus' sayings found in the "Q" source and places them after the Beatitudes and the woes. Jesus expounds on the central message of the reign of God. He exhorts his listeners to love their enemies, which includes those who hate them, curse them, and mistreat them. Instead of reacting violently against those who harm them, they must be willing to accept even greater injuries by turning the other cheek and not seeking a return from those who take from them. Jesus' teaching on love is radical, for he tells his disciples that they are to treat others the way they would want to be treated—how to love as God loves. Jesus says there is no difficulty in loving those who love us; even sinners do as much. To be called a true son or daughter of God, a person must be willing to imitate the love of God; for the Lord does not discriminate but loves those who are sinful and lacking gratitude for all good gifts coming from the Creator.

Luke links together random sayings of Jesus that speak of the mercy of God and the manner in which a true disciple imitates that mercy. A person will receive whatever judgment he or she passes on another. The one who condemns will be condemned, the one who forgives will be forgiven, and the one who gives will receive a great abundance in return. Commentators speculate that Luke is speaking to the leaders of the early Christian community when he warns against the blind leading the blind. All religious leaders of the community have no right to teach more than they have learned. If they do so, they are teaching their own blind message, which leads to disaster for the teacher and the follower. No disciple is superior to Jesus and his message, but the disciple who learns Jesus' message will be a true teacher of Jesus' message.

Jesus then turns his attention to the judgment of others. He teaches that hypocrites are often able to avoid seeing their own faults by making the faults of others appear greater than their own. Jesus knows human nature well when he warns his disciples against seeing the speck in a neighbor's eye while missing the larger fault ("the log") in one's own eye. He instructs his disciples to remove their own faults first in order to be able to guide their neighbors in removing the smaller faults in their life. Jesus teaches that just as a person can tell if a tree is healthy or decaying from the condition of the fruit it bears, so can a person judge a disciple by the type of life he or she lives. A good tree bears good fruit, and a bad tree bears rotten food. No one looks for figs (good fruit) among thorn bushes (bad tree), and no one expects to gather grapes (good fruit) from brambles (bad tree). In the same way, a person can expect others to act according to their basic attitude. A good person produces good fruit; and those who do evil, bad fruit.

Jesus calls his listeners to be strong in their faith. He tells them that people do not act as his followers simply by claiming to know all about him and his message; they must put this knowledge into practice. Those who put Jesus' message into action are like those who build their house (faith) on rock, while those who hear the words of Jesus and do not put them into practice build their house (faith) on a weak foundation, and they will fall at the sign of the first storm.

7:1–17 Healing and raising the dead

In this section of the gospel, Jesus heals the centurion's slave and raises a man from the dead. These two miracles are presented as two new types of miracles in Luke's Gospel, telling the story of a centurion pleading for the health of his slave. The story is similar to that found in the Gospel of Matthew, but Luke, with a special concern for those who do not belong to the Jewish people, makes some significant changes in his story.

In Luke's presentation, the centurion does not come to Jesus by himself but instead sends some leading Jewish friends to plead for the health of his servant. The centurion recognizes his position as an outsider, respecting the Jewish attitudes and customs toward those who are not Israelites. The Jewish elders who come to Jesus to plead the cause of the centurion praise him for his love of the Jewish people and his concern in building their synagogue for them.

As Jesus nears the home of the centurion, friends of the centurion come as emissaries to express the words of this Roman soldier, stating that he deems himself unworthy to have Jesus enter his home. The centurion was most likely conscious that Jesus would have become ritually unclean by entering the house of a Gentile. Jesus responds in amazement at the faith of the centurion, and as a result, the servant is healed. The central theme of the passage is not the healing but the faith shown by the centurion.

At the gate of the town of Nain, Jesus encounters a funeral procession in which a man, the only son of a widow, is being carried out for burial. The Lord exercised strong compassion for the woman by raising the man from the dead. Luke does not mention any sign of faith shown by the people before Jesus performs this miracle. In an Old Testament story that tells of Elijah staying with a widow whose son died, Elijah raises the son to life and gives him back to his mother (1 Kings 17:22–23). Luke alludes to this story when he describes Jesus raising the man and giving him to his mother. The crowd's response shows they recognize this as more than a mere healing miracle; it is a miracle that reflects an act of God in their midst. They respond with a type of awesome fear in the presence of God.

7:18–35 Testimony about John

The aforementioned stories of healing and raising the dead are Luke's way of setting the scene for what comes next. In this gospel passage, we hear about John's disciples who approach Jesus on the Baptist's behalf to inquire whether he is the one who is to come or if they should look for another. "The one who is to come" directly references the Book of Malachi (3:1).

John the Baptist, although he prepared the way for the Lord's coming, is portrayed here as uncertain as to whether Jesus was the true Messiah. Jesus not only teaches the disciples of John, but he also clarifies the Baptist's understanding of the Messiah. In Luke's presentation here, Jesus is curing the sick and casting out demons when John's disciples arrive. He tells them to return to their master and report what they have seen and heard, namely, that those who are blind see, those who are lame walk, those with leprosy are cleansed, and those who are poor have the Good News preached to them. These actions fulfill the prophetic message of Isaiah, foretelling signs of the messianic age and declaring that those who are blind will see and those who are deaf will hear (Isaiah 29:18; 35:5–6).

Jesus also proclaims that those who take no offense at him are blessed, accepting Jesus as the Messiah despite all previous expectations.

As the followers of John depart to bring Jesus' word to the Baptist, Jesus praises John, posing a rhetorical question to the people, "What did you go out to the desert to see—a reed swayed by the wind?...someone dressed in fine garments?...a prophet? (Luke 7:24–26). The answer, of course, is that they went out to see a prophet. Jesus tells them that John is more than an ordinary prophet. He is the one foretold by Isaiah (40:3), who spoke of a messenger sent by God to prepare the way for the coming of the Lord. Jesus declares that John is greater than those born of a woman, but the least in the kingdom of God is greater than he. Those who share in Jesus' gift of baptism share in the reign of God, a gift extending beyond natural birth and death.

The sinners and outcasts who accepted John's baptism show pleasure at the words of Jesus concerning John. However, the Pharisees and lawyers who had rejected the preaching and baptism of John show their displeasure. Jesus has harsh words for those who have rejected his and John's message. He compares the Pharisees to children who do not know what they want. They do not dance when they hear joyful music (they rejected Jesus who came eating and drinking). They refuse to mourn when they hear a dirge (they rejected John who came neither eating nor drinking). In this gospel account, the Jewish people rejected God's plan. Jesus' words are harsh toward the Pharisees who refuse to accept the message of these important prophets in their midst. They call John mad for his ascetic way of life, and they label Jesus a glutton because of his call to share in the Good News. God's wisdom is fully realized by those who accept Jesus' message.

Review Questions

1. Is it possible to follow Jesus' message to love our enemies? If so, explain.
2. What repercussions occur when we judge others? Why does Jesus teach us not to judge?
3. How does building our faith on a firm foundation help us to bear good fruit?
4. Why are the healing of the centurion's servant and the raising of the widow's son from the dead important lessons for us?

Closing Prayer (SEE PAGE 14)

Pray the closing prayer now or after *lectio divina*.

Lectio Divina (SEE PAGE 7)

Relax your body and maintain a posture of prayer (back straight, eyes shut, feet flat on the floor). This exercise can take as long as you want, but in the context of this Bible study, 10 to 20 minutes should be sufficient.

The meditations that follow are provided only to help group participants use this prayer form, but note that *lectio* is intended to bring one to a place of prayerful contemplation where the Word of God speaks to the hearer from his or her heart. (See page 7 for further instruction.)

Living as a follower of Jesus (6:27–49)

In 1960, Pope John XXIII convened the Second Vatican Council destining to bring the Church into the modern era. He built the council on a firm foundation of faith, showing love among friends and enemies, refusing to judge others, and welcoming all people to share in God's love. Imitating the attitude of Pope John XXIII, who gave an example of the attitude of Christ in our world today, is a challenge for all of us.

✠ *What can I learn from this passage?*

Healing and raising the dead (7:1–17)

The healing of the centurion's slave shows that Jesus can heal without being present with the person needing healing. The raising of the widow's son illustrates how a compassionate God often brings healing into our lives without us first asking for it. In these miracles, Jesus reveals the mind and actions of God.

✠ *What can I learn from this passage?*

Testimony about John (7:18–35)

Jesus, the Son of God, and John the Baptist, a holy prophet, lived different types of spirituality. Jesus did not fast, as we read in the previous passage in Luke's Gospel, and John the Baptist is portrayed here as fasting from food and drink often. Though the Son of God and the Baptist expressed

---

their spirituality in two different ways, each fulfilled a special mission in creation. A person's spiritual motive is important, not just his or her actions.

✠ *What can I learn from this passage?*

PART 2: INDIVIDUAL STUDY (LUKE 7:36—8:56)

Day 1: The Penitent Woman (7:36—8:3)

Jesus came for the salvation of all people, and though this gospel emphasizes Jesus' love for the outcasts and downtrodden, we will also glimpse him ministering to the Jewish people as he does with the Pharisees. Luke describes one such meal with a Pharisee named Simon who invited Jesus to dine with him 7:36ff, 11:37ff, and 14:1ff). In Jesus' day, people reclined at table, resting on their sides and elbows, instead of sitting in chairs. In this posture, the feet of Jesus and the others at table would be easily accessible to anyone who wished to wash the person's feet.

While Jesus is dining with Simon, a woman known as a sinner comes into the banquet and anoints Jesus' feet with oil, washing them with her tears, and drying them with her hair. Some writers believe this woman is Mary Magdalene or Mary, the sister of Martha, but there is no evidence about the woman's identity. Simon, true to the gospel image of the Pharisees, believes that a good person would not allow a sinful person to touch him or her. Because of this, he presumes that Jesus lacks knowledge of this woman's sinfulness, thus accusing Jesus in his mind and heart of not being a prophet.

Jesus reads Simon's thoughts and responds with a short parable about a rich moneylender and two debtors. One of the debtors owed five hundred days' wages and the other owed fifty. The moneylender forgives both debts. Jesus asks Simon which of the two debtors was more grateful to the lender. Simon reluctantly answers in favor of the one who has received forgiveness for the greater debt. Jesus then compares Simon's lack of concern for Jesus with the woman's obvious concern and love for him.

In Jesus' era, when a guest came into a house for dinner, the host would usually have a servant wash his feet. The host then welcomed the guest with a kiss and had the guest's head anointed. Simon did not have Jesus' feet washed and he did not receive him with the customary kiss and anointing. The woman, however, used her tears to wash Jesus' feet, kissed them, and anointed them. Because she had many sins, she had a greater need to express her love and gratitude. Her great faith enabled Jesus to forgive her sins. When Jesus tells her that her sins are forgiven, the other guests wonder who it is that can forgive sins. Jesus praises her faith, and using the common bidding of the day, he tells her to go in peace.

After speaking of the woman who washed Jesus' feet, Luke speaks of other women who follow Jesus. As Jesus continues his journey, preaching about the kingdom of God in towns and villages, the Twelve and some women whom Jesus cured of evil spirits or infirmities accompany him. Luke mentions the names of several of these women, two of whom, Mary Magdalene and Joanna, will be witnesses to the empty tomb at the time of Jesus' resurrection. During the time of Jesus, women were considered inferior to men, and although they would on occasion accompany the men on their journeys, writers would ordinarily not mention them.

Lectio Divina

Spend 8 to 10 minutes in silent contemplation of the following passage:

> We may never see the sinner change interiorly, but we do not have the right to judge the spiritual condition of another. Many sinners have eventually become great saints.

✠ *What can I learn from this passage?*

Day 2: The Parable of the Sower (8:4–15)

Luke follows Mark closely in presenting the parable of the sower, but he ends the story differently. In the Gospel of Mark, sowing on good soil results in a yield of thirty, sixty, or a hundredfold. Jesus tells of a sower who sowed his seed on a path, on rocky ground, and among thorns, only to have the seed destroyed and bear no fruit. Some seed falls on good ground and produces fruit a hundredfold. Luke speaks only of a yield of a hundredfold, omitting Mark's reference to the thirty or sixtyfold. Jesus ends by saying that those who have ears to hear should understand what he is teaching.

When Jesus ends the parable, the disciples ask him to explain it to them. Jesus tells his disciples that he speaks in parables so that others will not understand his message, as foretold by Isaiah (6:9). Jesus' words indicate in actuality that the people themselves have chosen to close their ears to understanding the message of Jesus. For many of those who do not believe, the Word of God does not take root and therefore they are unable to understand Jesus' parables, lacking the "ears to hear."

The meaning of the seed becomes confusing. Luke first declares that the seed is the Word of God that falls on different parts of the ground. He then changes the seed from the Word of God to the person who is receiving the Word. The seed that falls on the path are those who hear God's word, but the devil, like the birds of the air, comes and snaps it up. The seed that falls on rocky ground refers to those who receive the Word joyfully but, lacking any root, fall away at the first temptation. The seed that falls among the thorns are like those who receive the Word, soon smothered and destroyed by worldly concerns and pleasures. The seed on good ground indicates those who persevere, living a life open to the Word of God, and producing a magnificent harvest.

Lectio Divina

Spend 8 to 10 minutes in silent contemplation of the following passage:

> For most of us, our faith comes as a tiny seed planted in our heart. Faith, like love, never stands still. Love either grows or diminishes, depending on our nourishing of that gift. The seed of faith demands that we keep nourishing it so that it takes root and grows in our heart instead of being choked and smothered by the cares of the world.

✠ *What can I learn from this passage?*

Day 3: The Lamp Under a Basket (8:16–21)

Jesus' parable about the lamp on the lampstand addresses the mission of the disciples of Jesus. They must let the Good News they hear from Jesus light up the world, one that is not hidden but gives light to all who see it. After the resurrection of Jesus, the disciples will share his message with the whole world as though they are sharing light in the darkness. Nothing about the reign of God will remain unknown. Those who hear Jesus' Word and share it with others will continue to grow in understanding, while those who receive this message and refuse to share it with others will lose it.

Luke, avoiding Jesus' apparent rejection of his family as found in the Gospel of Mark, simply tells us that the family of Jesus could not reach him because of the large crowd. Mark mentions that Jesus' family thought he was mad. Like Mark, Luke uses the occasion to have Jesus teach a message about a true spiritual relationship with him. Those who hear the Word of God and live it are true members of Jesus' family. Jesus is not rejecting his family but expanding it to include everyone who is faithful to him.

Lectio Divina

Spend 8 to 10 minutes in silent contemplation of the following passage:

Jesus is the light of the world who shares his light with his disciples. Jesus no longer walks this earth in human form, but his light continues to shine in all those who live with faith in Jesus' message. Jesus, the light of the world, was not merely an event that lasted thirty-three years, but an event that lights up the world until the end of time. Christians have the duty of keeping the flame of Christ alive in every era of creation.

✠ *What can I learn from this passage?*

Day 4: The Calming of the Storm at Sea (8:22–25)

The miracle of calming the storm while at sea is the first of four miracles Luke introduces. Jesus directs his disciples to cross the sea to the other side, and during the journey, he falls asleep. A treacherous storm erupts, and the boat is in danger of sinking. In a panic, the disciples awaken Jesus and yell to him that they are in danger. They address him as "Master" rather than "Lord," showing that they do not cry out with faith but with the attitude of disciples addressing their leader. Jesus rebukes the storm, and all becomes calm. In Jesus' day, many believed that the sea was the abode of demons and that the storm came from the angry activity of the demons of the deep. The gospel writers do not simply tell us that Jesus calmed the storm but that he rebuked the storm, in the same way that he rebuked the unclean spirits. For the people of Jesus' day, his calming of the storm would be seen as power over demons.

After calming the storm, Jesus asks the disciples about their faith. They had already shown their lack of faith by addressing Jesus as "Master," and Jesus challenges them to consider their lack of faith. The disciples are so astounded at Jesus' act of divine power that they do not answer him. Power over the seas belongs to God alone, as shown in the story of creation when God puts order into the watery mass (Genesis 1:2ff). The disciples wonder who this person is who can command the wind and the sea.

Lectio Divina

Spend 8 to 10 minutes in silent contemplation of the following passage:

> When a woman was visiting a well-loved and deeply spiritual forty-year-old woman who was dying of cancer, she asked her, "Why you?" The dying woman answered, "Why not me?" She did not believe God owed her anything for all she had done. She taught people to trust God, even when tragedies happen.

✠ *What can I learn from this passage?*

Day 5: The Healing of the Man Possessed by a Demon (8:26–39)

Jesus travels to the country of the Gerasenes, a place outside Jewish territory. A naked man who was possessed by a demon and who lived among the tombs immediately recognizes Jesus and, falling down before him, asks in a loud voice what Jesus has to do with him. Luke gives the impression that the demon rather than the man is speaking. The demon identifies Jesus as Son of the Most High God and shows his inability to ignore Jesus. Recognizing Jesus' power over him, he begs Jesus not to torment him. Luke portrays the exorcism of the evil spirit from the man as a means of tormenting the evil spirits. The demon had such great control over the man that the man would have to be bound by chains, but even so the man would break the chains and the evil spirit would drive the man into "deserted places."

Luke shows the control Jesus has over the demon by having him honestly answer Jesus' questions. When Jesus asks the demon its name, it tells Jesus its name is "Legion," a term used to refer to a group of several thousand soldiers. In ancient Jewish belief, the ability to know the true identity of someone gave the person who knew the other's identity power over him or her. The name indicates that many demons possessed the man. They begged Jesus to send them into a herd of swine that was feeding nearby rather than have them depart into the abyss, which the people of Jesus' day saw as a dismal place of demons. At the request of the demons, Jesus casts them into a herd of swine, but the swine rush into the lake and drown, thus hurling the demons into the abyss. By the visible exit of the demons in the swine, Luke is telling us that Jesus has cleared the land of demons.

When the people of the area hear what happened and come to Jesus, they find the formerly possessed man sitting at the feet of Jesus, a way of portraying the man as a disciple of Jesus. When the townspeople saw that the man was clothed and healthy, they feared Jesus, believing he could be a greater demon than the ones cast out, and they beg him to leave their territory. Jesus and his disciples get into the boat and leave. Although the man who was saved from the demons wants to go with him, Jesus tells him to remain in the territory to spread word about the event. The man becomes a true disciple by spreading word about the deed to the whole town. Jesus has no need to protect his identity as the Messiah in this passage, since he is no longer in Jewish territory and the people of the area had no expectations of a warrior messiah.

Lectio Divina

Spend 8 to 10 minutes in silent contemplation of the following passage:

Because evil is such a disruption of good, it gains headlines in our newspapers, leading people to ask, "Why is there so much evil in the world?" The reality, however, is that without all the goodness in the world, we would never recognize evil. Some people, like the people of the town of the possessed man, fear faith in Jesus, since he helped them recognize the battle against evil in the world.

✠ *What can I learn from this passage?*

Day 6: Raising a Girl to Life and Curing a Woman (8:40–56)

Luke continues to stress Jesus' popularity with the crowd by stating that the crowd was waiting for him when he returned to the other side. Luke follows Mark closely in his presentation of the two healing stories that follow, namely, the healing of the woman with the hemorrhage and the raising of the daughter of Jairus from the dead. He uses the same technique used by Mark in sandwiching one story inside the other.

Although Jesus experienced confrontations from many of the religious leaders of the people, some pious Jews believed in Jesus. In this passage, a leader of the synagogue named Jairus comes to Jesus and begs him to come to his house and heal his dying twelve-year-old daughter. Jesus agrees to come to the house of the synagogue leader, and Luke mentions that the crowd with Jesus had grown so large that it was crushing him. The gospel writer presents this piece of information to prepare the reader for the following healing.

On Jesus' way to the house of the synagogue leader, a woman, who has had a hemorrhage for twelve years and spent all she had on doctors without any cure, comes up behind Jesus and touches the fringe of his cloak. She is immediately healed. When Jesus feels the power go out of him, he asks who touched him. Peter, not knowing what happened, treats his question as a foolish one as they were in the midst of a crushing crowd. Jesus declares that he knows someone touched him, since he felt power go out of him. The woman, trembling at being discovered, admits she is the one, and in front of all tells of her healing. Jesus does not tell her that her faith has healed her but rather that her faith has saved her.

The gospel writer is following the custom of the day in linking a healing with salvation. Jesus bids her to go in peace. The message of the story is that it is the faith of the person seeking the cure that enables it to take place. Jesus did not intentionally cure her, since he was unaware of her presence. Unlike Jesus' visit to Nazareth where his neighbors lacked faith, it was the woman's great faith that brought her healing and salvation.

The gospel writer returns to the story of Jairus, whose faith is about to be challenged. Someone from the official's household arrives and reports that the girl has died, but Jesus bids Jairus to have faith and believe that his daughter will be saved. At the house, Jesus orders the mourners to stop their weeping and declares that the girl is only sleeping. The mourners, certain that the girl is dead, scoff at Jesus.

As Jesus enters the house, he takes the parents of the child with him, along with Peter, John, and James, the three disciples who will accompany him at the transfiguration and during the agony in the garden. Their presence in this passage tells the reader something significant is about to happen. Jesus takes the girl by the hand, raises her to life, and directs them to give her something to eat.

The early Church referred to a dead person as being asleep in the Lord, awaiting the day of resurrection. When Jesus declared that the girl was asleep, the gospel writers were most likely alluding to this manner of speaking of death used in the early Church. A sign of good health in Jesus' day was the ability to eat. Since Jesus had returned to Jewish territory, he instructed the parents of the girl to tell no one about the event.

Lectio Divina

Spend 8 to 10 minutes in silent contemplation of the following passage:

At one point in the Scriptures, Jesus tells us that if we have faith, we can move mountains. These stories of the faith of the woman seeking a healing and the synagogue leader illustrate Jesus' message. Faith allows God to act in a person's life, in whatever way God wills. Faith and trust in the will of God are the foundation of Jesus' miraculous deeds. They can move mountains.

✠ *What can I learn from this passage?*

Review Questions

1. What can we learn by contrasting Simon, the Pharisee, with the repentant woman who bathed and anointed the feet of Jesus?
2. How can we apply the story of the sower to some situations in our world today?
3. Why is Jesus' message about the lamp important for our lives as Christians?
4. What messages do we find in the stories of Jairus' daughter and the woman with a hemorrhage?

LESSON 5

Passion, Death, and Resurrection Predicted

LUKE 9:1–10:42

You shall love the Lord, your God, with all your heart, with all your being, with all your strength, and with all your mind, and your neighbor as yourself (10:27).

Opening Prayer (SEE PAGE 14)

Context

Part 1: Luke 9:1–50 Jesus sends the Twelve on a mission with a sense of urgency. Meanwhile, Herod wonders about the identity of Jesus. Jesus feeds the five thousand in the desert, and Peter professes that Jesus is the Messiah of God. Jesus predicts his passion and lists the conditions necessary for discipleship. He is transfigured before his disciples, and when he comes down the mountain, he casts a demon out of a boy. Jesus continues to teach his disciples about the kingdom of God, exhorting them not to seek places of worldly honor.

Part 2: Luke 9:51–10:42 Jesus begins his journey to Jerusalem. He refuses to punish the Samaritans for rejecting him and his disciples, explaining the radical dedication needed to become one of his followers. He sends seventy-two disciples on a mission and reproaches the unrepentant towns. Jesus thanks the Father for revealing his message to the little ones (his disciples). He agrees with a scholar of the Law who proclaims the greatest commandment, explaining it further with the parable of the Good Samaritan. Jesus visits Martha and Mary and declares that Mary has chosen the better part by sitting at his feet.

PART 1: GROUP STUDY (LUKE 9:1–50)

Read aloud Luke 9:1–50.

9:1–17 The mission of the Twelve

Jesus prepares the Twelve for the ministry ahead. In this passage, the preparation of the Twelve not only involves spreading Jesus' message but also implicitly refers to the role of the Twelve in sharing the Eucharist with the crowds. Jesus first calls the disciples to share in his ministry by giving them power over demons, which means they share in God's authority over unclean spirits. They are then sent out with the mission of preaching the kingdom of God and healing the sick.

On their journey, they should take nothing for their own comfort—no traveling bag, no food, no money, and only a single tunic—and they are to trust that the people they serve will supply their needs. The Twelve are to shake the dust off their feet if the people of a particular town do not accept them. This is a sign that the people have rejected the message of God delivered by the Twelve. They set out, traveling as Jesus did, from village to village, spreading the Good News and healing the sick.

As the reputation of Jesus spread, Herod, who had John the Baptist killed, hears that some were saying that Jesus is John raised from the dead. Others were asking if Elijah had come, while still others stated that one of the ancient prophets had arisen. In Mark's Gospel, Herod believes it is John who is raised from the dead, while Luke pictures Herod as confused and expressing no opinion. This short passage about Herod introduces a series of episodes that attempt to answer Herod's question about the identity of Jesus.

The Apostles return, excited over the outcome of their mission. In the Gospel of Mark, Jesus takes his Apostles to a deserted place. In Luke, Jesus takes his Apostles to a town called Bethsaida, the hometown of some of the Apostles. Although the Apostles have begun to share in Jesus' preaching and healing, the crowd still seeks out Jesus, who continues his ministry.

As evening approaches, the Twelve advise Jesus to send the people away so they can get some food. Jesus urges them to feed the crowd, but the Twelve protest that they have only five loaves of bread and two fish. A tone of sarcasm enters the story as the Apostles ask Jesus if they should go and buy enough food for the multitude, which the Evangelist tells us amounted to five thousand men (plus the uncounted women and children).

Jesus directs his Apostles to divide the crowd into groups of fifty each. He then blesses the bread and the fish. The manner in which he performs this function reflects the rite of the eucharistic celebration used in the early Church. Jesus does not distribute the food, but gives it to his Apostles to distribute. In this way, the reader understands that the ministry of an apostle includes the ministry of the Word and the Eucharist. Whenever God gives us gifts, we always receive an overabundance, as noted by the twelve baskets of food left over. The number twelve reminds the reader of the twelve tribes of Israel. The miracle is performed for a Jewish audience in Jewish territory.

9:18–27 Peter's profession of faith and discipleship

Luke again reminds us of the important part prayer plays at decisive moments in Jesus' life. In the midst of his prayer, Jesus asks his disciples an important question, "Who do the crowds say that I am?" We have already seen that some thought Jesus was Elijah, while others (Herod) thought he might be John the Baptist raised from the dead. Peter, speaking on behalf of the disciples, tells Jesus that they believe he is "the Messiah of God." Since the people of Jesus' day would not understand the true meaning of *messiah,* Jesus forbids his disciples to spread word about his identity.

Jesus links the true meaning of Messiah with his passion, death, and resurrection, which he predicts immediately after Peter's profession of faith. Luke omits the account found in the other synoptic gospels that tells of Peter's rejection of Jesus' prediction of his passion, death, and resurrection and Jesus' harsh rebuke of Peter. This omission may have as its source Luke's great respect for Peter, the head of the Apostles. Once Jesus establishes that he will suffer, die, and be raised, he then calls his disciples to follow him by being willing to suffer for the sake of the kingdom, no matter what the cost. They must take up their cross and follow him. Luke adds the word *daily,* which emphasizes that the disciple must be a follower of Christ at every moment.

When Jesus says that those who wish to save their lives will lose it, he is referring to disciples who deny Christ. Jesus adds that those who truly wish to save their lives for all eternity must be willing to forgo a desire to obtain worldly rewards. From an eternal viewpoint, there is no profit in gaining the whole world and losing one's eternal life. Jesus said that one should worship the Lord God alone; the true disciple must remain faithful to Jesus. If a person denies Jesus in the face of persecution, Jesus states that he will deny that person before God the Father.

When Jesus refers to himself as the "Son of Man" in this passage, he is using the term as a messianic title. Jesus declares that some will not die until they see the kingdom of God. In doing this, he is referring to those who will experience the beginning of the kingdom of God in the early Church community after Jesus' resurrection. Some commentators believe Luke is referring to the time after the destruction of Jerusalem (70) when Christianity became distinct from the official Judaism of the day.

9:28–36 The transfiguration

Luke sets the scene for the transfiguration of Jesus with several signs, indicating he is about to present a major message of the gospel. The first sign a major event is about to take place rests with the three disciples Jesus chooses to accompany him. Peter, James, and John were with Jesus when he raised the daughter of Jairus from the dead, and they will be with him later during the agony in the garden.

A second noteworthy sign is that Jesus takes them up a mountain with him, the typical Old Testament place of God's visitation with the Chosen People. A third sign of the importance of the transfiguration about to take place is that Luke portrays Jesus as going up the mountain to pray. Luke continues to show that Jesus prays before important events in his life. Unlike the writers of the Gospels of Mark and Matthew, who place the event on the sixth day after choosing his disciples, Luke places it eight days later.

On the mountain during prayer, Jesus' face changes in appearance and his clothes become dazzling white. Moses, who represents the Law of the Old Testament, and Elijah, who represents the prophets of the Old Testament, appear with Jesus and talk with him about the exodus he was going to accomplish in Jerusalem, a reference to his passion, death, and resurrection. Jesus' transfiguration is a sharp contrast to the prediction of his passion and death and the call to his disciples to accept their cross and follow him. Jesus, in the glory of the transfiguration, gives his disciples a glimpse of the glory that is to come in his resurrection. His saving action comes not only by way of his passion and death but through his resurrection as well. The presence of Moses and Elijah with Jesus shows him to be the fulfillment of the Law and the Prophets.

Peter, with his usual impetuosity, wishes to build three dwellings, one for Jesus, one for Moses, and one for Elijah. This could be a reference to the Jewish feast of Tabernacles, a harvest feast commemorating a time when the pilgrims to Jerusalem lived in tents. In the Exodus, a cloud overshadowed the tent of the Lord whenever the presence of God entered it. A cloud overshadows them in this transfiguration experience, and a voice from the cloud proclaims, as it did at Jesus' baptism, that Jesus is God's chosen Son. The voice urges the disciples to listen to Jesus' message. The transfiguration ends abruptly with dramatic silence pervading the scene, and the disciples tell no one of their experience.

9:37–50 Jesus comes down the mountain

Jesus comes down the mountain to the daily world of his disciples, but he finds them lacking the faith necessary to cast a demon out of a boy and the ability to understand the meaning of his passion, death, and resurrection. He admonishes them to live with the humility of a child and that all those who minister in his name do not necessarily belong to their company.

When Jesus and the three disciples come down the mountain, they are met by a man who begs Jesus to heal his only son from the power of an evil spirit. The boy's ailments of seizures, screams, convulsion, and foaming at the mouth that leave the boy exhausted sound a great deal like epilepsy. The disciples of Jesus, despite their successful mission of preaching and healing at an earlier time, are not able to cast the evil spirit out of the boy.

A frustrated Jesus scolds the crowd for their unbelief. When they bring the boy before Jesus, the boy reacts in a manner similar to previous expulsions of demons. The demon throws the boy to the ground in a convulsion, and Jesus rebukes the unclean spirit, curing the boy and giving him back to his father. Luke mentions that Jesus returned the boy to his father, as though the boy, possessed by the demon, no longer belonged to the father until Jesus cured him. The people are amazed at the power of God shown through Jesus.

Jesus again predicts his passion and resurrection, but his disciples still do not understand what he is telling them. Luke implies that they cannot understand the message of Jesus' passion because it has been hidden by God. True understanding will only come after they experience and understand the eventual resurrection of Jesus. The disciples are afraid to ask Jesus about his prediction.

Another sign that they misunderstand Jesus' identity and mission occurs as the disciples discuss who will be the greatest in the kingdom. Jesus uses a little child to teach a lesson. The one who accepts anyone who is as unimportant as a child, for the sake of Jesus, accepts not only Jesus but the One who sent him. Thus the most insignificant among the disciples is the greatest, according to Jesus.

John the Apostle misunderstands Jesus' message in this account, for he tells Jesus that they tried to stop a man from expelling demons in Jesus' name because he was not one of the disciples traveling with them. Jesus corrects his followers, teaching them that anyone who does not act contrary to the mission of the disciples actually belongs to their company.

Review Questions

1. What is the message of Jesus' feeding the five thousand?
2. How does the call to discipleship reflect Jesus' prediction of his passion?
3. What is significant about the transfiguration of Jesus?

Closing Prayer (SEE PAGE 14)

Pray the closing prayer now or after *lectio divina*.

Lectio Divina (SEE PAGE 7)

Relax your body and maintain a posture of prayer (back straight, eyes shut, feet flat on the floor). This exercise can take as long as you want, but in the context of this Bible study, 10 to 20 minutes should be sufficient.

The meditations that follow are provided only to help group participants use this prayer form, but note that *lectio* is intended to bring one to a place of prayerful contemplation where the Word of God speaks to the hearer from his or her heart. (See page 7 for further instruction.)

The mission of the Twelve (9:1–17)

The Twelve represent the Church, and the ministry of the Twelve is our ministry as Church. The Church has the mission of having authority over demons, proclaiming the presence of the reign of God, and bringing healing to the spiritually and physically ill. Although Jesus commissions the Twelve in this passage, he expects all members of the Church to fulfill the mission of bringing Christ's mercy and love to the world.

The Church also has the mission of sharing Christ's message and providing the Eucharist for God's people. As members of the Church, the body of Christ on Earth, we are called to be a eucharistic people; overcoming evil with good, healing the sick, comforting the dying, spreading Christ's message, and sharing in the banquet of Christ's Body and Blood in the Eucharist.

✠ *What can I learn from this passage?*

Peter's profession of faith and discipleship (9:18–27)

Commitments may be easily created, but living up to one's commitment becomes a real challenge. Through our baptism and participation in the Eucharist, we commit ourselves as disciples of Jesus. But Jesus warns that this commitment means picking up our cross daily. At times, we may wish that the demands of this cross could pass from us. Yet, like Jesus, we pray that we will have the courage and dedication to live our commitment to accept God's will to the very end of our lives.

✠ *What can I learn from this passage?*

The transfiguration (9:28–36)

After the Apostles view Jesus in his glory, they hear the message that is addressed to all of us, "This is my chosen Son; listen to him." The voice is telling us to listen to Jesus as he speaks to us in prayer and in the Scriptures. God invites us to recognize the glory of Christ and Christ's words so that we can fall silent and listen to him.

✠ *What can I learn from this passage?*

Jesus comes down the mountain (9:37–50)

Jesus' disciples want to control everything, even to the point of seeking to control those who can share Christ's gifts with others. In reality, they are still controlled by worldly attitudes of life. They have a great deal to learn before they can become faithful and committed followers of Christ. The challenge continues even today.

✠ *What can I learn from this passage?*

PART 2: INDIVIDUAL STUDY (LUKE 9:51—10:42)

Day 1: The Demands of Discipleship (9:51–62)

In the following passages we see Jesus' ministry move beyond Galilee toward Jerusalem, the holy city and the place of fulfillment for all the great prophets of Israel. Luke recognizes the importance of Jerusalem for the message of Jesus, and he structures his gospel in such a way that Jesus makes only one journey toward Jerusalem during his public ministry. Jesus most likely made more than one trip to this holy city during his ministry, but in this gospel this single journey is a dramatic event that leads toward Jesus' passion, death, resurrection, and ascension. Commentators call this section the long interpolation, as much of the material in these chapters is found only in the Gospel of Luke.

At the beginning of his public ministry, Jesus was rejected by his own townspeople. Now at the beginning of this major journey toward Jerusalem, Jesus faces another form of rejection. The Jews and the Samaritans had lived for many centuries with religious and political differences and a deep hatred for one another. The Samaritans rejected all Jews heading toward the holy city of Jerusalem, so when the disciples go ahead of Jesus to prepare the way for his passage through Samaria, they refuse to welcome Jesus and his disciples. James and John react by asking Jesus if they should call fire from heaven to destroy these people. As their request for vengeance from heaven greatly exceeds the rebuff they experienced from the Samaritans, Jesus scolds them for their lack of tolerance.

Next, Luke provides a lesson on deep commitment and the demands of discipleship. On the journey, when a man asks to follow Jesus, Jesus teaches him about mission and the way of a would-be follower. Unlike the animals (foxes and birds), the disciple must live like the Son of Man, with nowhere to rest. The call to discipleship demands immediate and total commitment. When Jesus invites another man to follow him, the man wishes to return home and bury his father. The desire to bury his father does not mean his father is dying; he is really asking Jesus to wait for the day when his father dies and he is free to follow.

Jesus' response that "the dead should bury the dead" is referring to those who are dead to Jesus' message and filled with worldly concerns. Those called by Jesus should be willing to leave all, even family, to become his disciple. Another wishes to bid farewell to his family, but Jesus warns that anyone who looks back to the concerns of the world is unfit for discipleship. In the Old Testament, Elijah allows Elisha to return home to bid farewell to his family (1 Kings 19:19–21), but Elisha immediately returns to Elijah and dedicates himself to his mission. Jesus, who apparently has left all for the sake of the reign of God, asks his disciples to do the same.

Lectio Divina

Spend 8 to 10 minutes in silent contemplation of the following passage:

When many see evil in the world, they wonder why God does not destroy the evildoer. Jesus, who is God, loves everyone and did not come to destroy the sinner but to give the sinner every opportunity for salvation. Followers of Jesus must develop the attitude of Jesus, who allows sinners time to change their lives.

✠ *What can I learn from this passage?*

Day 2: Second Mission of the Disciples (10:1–16)

Luke alone mentions a second mission for the followers of Jesus. In an earlier passage, Luke describes Jesus sending out the Twelve on their mission (9:1–6), and now he speaks of sending out seventy-two disciples ahead of him in pairs to all the towns and places he intends to visit. Just as Jesus sent messengers into Samaria to prepare his way, he now sends his disciples ahead of him to prepare the people for his coming.

It was customary in Jesus' day for a well-known person of importance to send emissaries ahead to prepare for the person's coming. Jesus speaks of a plentiful harvest with few laborers. The harvest referred to here is one of people, as Jesus needs laborers to bring his message to the multitudes. He urges his disciples to pray that the master of the harvest (God) will send laborers into the fields. Luke gives Jesus' directive to all disciples of every age, who must pray for this need.

The disciples are to travel as lambs among wolves, with little or no earthly possessions. In Isaiah (53:7), we read that the suffering servant (often seen as a reference to Jesus) was "like a lamb led to slaughter or a sheep silent before shearers, he did not open his mouth." A sense of urgency is again presented as the disciples are described as greeting no one and going without even the basic necessities: traveling bag, sandals, money bag. Christ's peace will accompany all who receive them. They are instructed to remain with the first household that receives them and not move from house to house. Their journey is not for leisure or visiting with friends but one centered on preaching Jesus' message. Because they are sharing the message of Jesus, their labors are worth the wages they receive, namely, food and lodging.

If a town rejects them, they are to shake the dust of that town from their feet, forgetting the area and moving forward in their mission. They are to cure the sick and preach about the kingdom of God. Those who listen to the message of the disciples are listening to Jesus, as those who reject them here also denounce the message of Christ. Jesus exhorts that Sodom (considered ungodly in the Book of Genesis) and pagan areas such as Tyre and Sidon (also in the Old Testament) would be better off than Chorazin and Bethsaida (cities near Jerusalem) on the day of judgment, as the people of Tyre and Sidon would have repented if they had seen the works of Jesus performed in their midst. Even Capernaum, the city Jesus used as the base for his ministry, would not share in his glory if they were to decline the message. Jesus declares that those who listen to his disciples are heeding his word, thus identifying himself with the ministry and work of his followers.

Lectio Divina

Spend 8 to 10 minutes in silent contemplation of the following passage:

> When Jesus speaks of laborers in his harvest, he is not restricting his message to those who are ordained or who belong to religious life. Rather, he is speaking to all those who choose to follow him, whatever their calling in life may be. The harvest refers to all people who need to hear the Word of God or who have heard God's Word but needs help assimilating it.

> ✠ *What can I learn from this passage?*

Day 3: The Joy of Discipleship (10:17–24)

The joyful disciples return after their mission, celebrating their power over demons. They tell Jesus that the demons were subject to them in his name. Jesus shares their joy, telling them that he saw Satan falling from heaven like lightning. Many pagans during Jesus' era believed that those who controlled the heavens also reigned over Earth, and Satan falling from the heavens signified his loss of control over Earth. Jesus' words are also a reference to the expected battle that some in Jesus' day believed would take place in the last days: the heavenly hosts will fight one another, and evil will be overpowered. The presence of the reign of God in the world is leading to the defeat of the kingdom of Satan. Jesus is telling his listeners that the battle has already begun.

Luke gives us an insight into Jesus' prayer as Jesus, also overwhelmed with joy, praises God, whom he addresses as "Father." God has allowed these disciples, referred to as "children," to receive a gift of faith that has been hidden from the wise and the clever. Many people of faith were not as well educated as those who denied Jesus. But as a gift of God, they actually understood Jesus' message far more clearly. It is not by intelligence but by faith that they are able to know the true identity of Jesus. This is the will of God, that people of faith should know God better.

By the will of the Father, everything now rests in the hands of the Son. The Father and Son share a mutual knowledge of each other, and a share in this knowledge is given to those chosen by the Son to receive it. Jesus reminds the disciples of the great gift they have received. They are blessed because they have been chosen to see and hear what great prophets and kings of the past longed to experience. Throughout the passage, Jesus does not praise the disciples for what they have done but gives praise to God for sharing this power with them. All that Jesus' disciples possess comes from God.

Lectio Divina

Spend 8 to 10 minutes in silent contemplation of the following passage:

Faith comes to us, not due to our intelligence, but as a gift from God. We, as disciples of Jesus, can rejoice when we are able to perform great deeds in Jesus' name. Yet God's greatest gift to us is that we share in the life and mission of Jesus.

✠ *What can I learn from this passage?*

Day 4: Love of God and the Good Samaritan (10:25–37)

A lawyer, a man well versed in Old Testament Scriptures, asks Jesus what he must do to gain eternal life. When Jesus asks the man what the Law says, the lawyer answers correctly by quoting from the Book of Deuteronomy (6:5), which calls for love of God, and from the Book of Leviticus (19:18), which invites us to love our neighbor. Jesus commends the insight of the lawyer. The Jewish people knew these laws, but it was only when Jesus came that these laws were conjoined. In the Gospel of Mark, Jesus makes this connection, but in Luke's Gospel, the lawyer makes the connection.

According to the Book of Leviticus, *neighbor* referred to another Israelite. The lawyer presses Jesus further by asking him to clarify who exactly is one's neighbor. In the story of the Good Samaritan, Jesus attempts to give him an insight into the meaning of neighbor as found in the Old

Testament. In this parable, a man is robbed, beaten, and left lying on the roadside. Those expected to help this unfortunate victim, a priest and a Levite, pass by without helping the man. Perhaps this avoidance refers to the Law indicating that they would be considered unclean by helping the man, especially if the man was covered with blood. The Law they practiced would have excused them for ignoring the man if he were a non-Jew, since they considered only Jews as their neighbors. Whatever the reason, the priest and the Levite pass on the opposite side of the road, as far away from the man as possible.

A Samaritan, a person who belonged to a group who was hated and avoided by the Jews, stops to care for the wounded man. He takes him to an inn, makes a deposit of two silver pieces, and promises the innkeeper that he will pay on his return journey whatever he owes for the care of this man. The story has a special sting for the Jews who could never imagine a Samaritan performing an act of kindness.

Jesus then turns to the lawyer and inquires which of the group of people in his story acted as a neighbor to the beaten man. The lawyer responds that the true neighbor was the one who treated the man with mercy. Jesus does not mean that only those who help others are neighbors to them but that everyone should have an attitude of being neighbors to all. The Samaritan saw himself as being a neighbor to the beaten man, as the merciful are those who recognize that they are truly neighbors to all, and all are neighbors to them. Jesus directs the lawyer to go and act in the same manner.

Lectio Divina

Spend 8 to 10 minutes in silent contemplation of the following passage:

A man offered a healthy kidney to anyone who needed one, even though the one receiving the kidney would be a stranger. When someone asked him how he could do this, his reply was, "After all, we're all brothers and sisters in the Lord." He eventually donated a kidney to a stranger who was a good match. Some, like the Samaritan, perform heroic acts because they view everyone as a neighbor in need.

✠ *What can I learn from this passage?*

Day 5: Martha and Mary (10:38–42)

On their journey, Jesus visits the home of a woman named Martha. Luke makes no immediate mention of Mary, the sister of Martha, who is also present in the story; yet she will appear as part of the central message of the passage. Martha is busy preparing the house for her guest while Mary sits at the feet of Jesus. When Martha complains, Jesus declares that Mary has chosen the better part, namely, to be present with him.

Many spiritual writers have used this passage as a sign that the contemplative life is more perfect than the active life. Some modern commentators have taken a different approach. In Jesus' day, women were not allowed to sit at the feet of a rabbi and learn. Martha could be complaining not that Mary is not serving Jesus as women were expected to do but that she is doing what women were forbidden to do. Jesus declares that Mary has chosen the better part by learning as a disciple rather than being worried about many things. Jesus did not condemn the active life in this passage nor did he have any intention of comparing the active with the contemplative life.

Lectio Divina

Spend 8 to 10 minutes in silent contemplation of the following passage:

> The story of Mary at the feet of Jesus may refer to her desire to learn from Jesus, or her contemplation of Jesus. Martha is not doing something bad; she is simply too busy to sit, learn, and contemplate at the feet of Jesus. Christ nourishes Martha by inviting her to begin spending some time sitting at his feet and contemplating the way of her special guest.

✠ *What can I learn from this passage?*

Review Questions

1. What is the central message of Jesus, who rebukes his disciples for wishing condemnation on the Samaritans for not welcoming them on the way to Jerusalem?
2. According to Jesus, who is truly wise and clever in God's eyes?
3. How can we apply the greatest commandment to our manner of life?
4. What do we learn from the story of Jesus' visit to Martha and Mary?

Jesus Accused of Being Possessed

LUKE 11:1—13:17

And I tell you, ask and you will receive; seek and you will find; knock and the door will be opened to you. For everyone who asks, receives; and the one who seeks, finds; and to the one who knocks, the door will be opened (11:9–10).

Opening Prayer (SEE PAGE 14)

Context

Part 1: Luke 11:1—12:12 Jesus teaches his disciples a lesson about prayer. When the religious leaders accuse Jesus of performing his deeds by the power of the prince of devils, Jesus points out how foolish this accusation is. He calls those who hear God's Word and respond to it as blessed, denounces the Pharisees, and warns the disciples about the persecution they must endure for his sake.

Part 2: Luke 12:13—13:17 Jesus points out how foolish it is to build up treasures for ourselves only on Earth. Christ acknowledges that he will be a cause of division in families, and he warns the people to recognize the signs of the times.

PART 1: GROUP STUDY (LUKE 11:1—12:12)

Read aloud Luke 11:1—12:12.

11:1–13 The Lord's Prayer

The role of a religious teacher was not only to teach the Law and the Prophets to his followers but also to teach them how to pray. After Jesus finished praying, one of his disciples asks him to teach them how to pray, as John the Baptist taught his disciples. Jesus teaches them a shorter version of the Lord's Prayer than the one found in the Gospel of Matthew. Many believe Luke's version of the prayer is closer to the original.

The prayer found in the Gospel of Luke begins simply with the word "Father." The term used by Jesus addresses God more intimately than would have been used by any pious Jew of that day. Jesus is sharing with his followers the intimacy he has with God. Jesus praises God's name, which, according to Jewish custom, was an indirect way of praising the person. He prays that the kingdom of God will be manifest and that God will provide one's daily needs.

The prayer for the forgiveness of sins requests that we be willing to forgive the sins of those who have hurt us, and the final petition prays that we might be freed from the daily trials of life that could turn us away from God. The ancient Israelites saw these tests as coming not only from Satan but also from God. Through testing, a person would show his or her worthiness for eternal life.

After Jesus teaches his disciples how to pray, he urges them to pray with perseverance. Jesus tells the parable of a man who unwillingly gets up from bed at night to give bread to a persistent neighbor just to get rid of him or her. The implication is that God, who is more generous and willing to respond than our neighbors, will certainly answer persistent prayer. Those who pray must remain constant in prayer. They must ask, seek, and knock to receive what they ask in prayer. Just as a father who is wicked will not offer his children something evil when they ask for something good, so God, who is all good and loves us, is willing to grant us an abundance of gifts when we pray with faith.

11:14–28 Jesus and Beelzebul

A common belief in Jesus' day was that Beelzebul, the prince of devils, had power over all evil spirits. The people also believed that many physical ailments were the result of an evil spirit within a person. When Jesus casts the evil spirit out of a man who cannot speak, the man regains his ability to speak. The crowd responds in two ways: first, by accusing Jesus of casting out devils by the power of evil (Beelzebul was a false god perceived as a representation of evil in ancient Judaism); second, the crowd sought more signs from Jesus before they were willing to believe.

Jesus answers their first question with the logical reply that a household divided against itself will be destroyed. If Satan (Beelzebul) is divided against Satan, then he will destroy himself. Since many of the Jewish healers of the day claimed to have power over demons, Jesus tells the people in the crowd that if they challenge his authority, they should in turn challenge the authority of these healers. If, however, Jesus casts out devils by the power of God, then the kingdom of God has truly arrived.

Jesus enforces his message with a parable. A strong man protects his property until a stronger man comes along, overpowers him, and takes possession of his arms and property. With Jesus, a person ministers either with him or against him.

Jesus delivers a second parable. When an unclean spirit leaves someone, it seeks others to inhabit, but finding none, it returns to the home from which it came. Finding the home (the person) swept and clean, the unclean spirit brings seven other spirits, more wicked than itself, who inhabit the person, thus making the last condition of the person worse than the first. All are called to live in accord with the spirit of the kingdom of God, and this must be done consciously as we must choose between God and Beelzebul.

Jesus' answer to his opponents draws words of praise from a woman in the crowd who praises the mother of Jesus for giving birth to him, declaring that the womb that bore him and the breasts that nursed him are blessed. Jesus answers that those who hear the Word of God and keep it are the ones who are truly blessed. In speaking this way, Jesus is not rejecting his mother. Rather, he is recognizing that she was willing to accept and live God's message in her life as all are called to do.

11:29–32 The demand for a sign

Besides accusing Jesus of casting out devils by the power of Beelzebul, the people ask for a sign. Jesus responds to their second request by stating that they are a wicked generation and that no sign but the sign of Jonah will be given. In the Old Testament story, the life and preaching of Jonah became a sign that leads the people of Nineveh to change their lives (Jonah 3:4–10). Just as Jonah spent three days and three nights in the belly of a great fish, so Jesus will remain in the tomb for three days before his resurrection. Jesus is speaking of his own passion and death. Although Jesus presents the sign of Jonah as an answer to the crowd, he realizes that the people will not understand this, and for this reason he can also say that no sign will be given. Because of their blindness, the people will not recognize the sign of Jonah.

In another Old Testament story, when the queen of the south hears of Solomon's wisdom, she visits him and praises the Lord for the abundance given to Solomon (1 Kings 10:1–13). Jesus warns the people that the people of Nineveh and the queen of the south will rise with this present generation, and they will condemn it. The people of Nineveh accepted the sign of Jonah, but the people of Jesus' day who had the Lord present refused to see who was before them.

11:33–54 Live in the light

A person lights a lamp to receive light, an image used in the New Testament to refer to Christ. In Jesus' day, many people believed the eye allowed light to enter a person. The blind person lived with darkness within and could see nothing because of this darkness. Jesus tells his listeners that they must let the light within them shine for the whole world to see. Once they reject darkness (evil) for the sake of the light (Christ), they will be able to reflect this light to the world.

A Pharisee invites Jesus to dine at his home. Jesus accepts the invitation and reclines at table to eat. During the meal, Jesus castigates the Pharisees with three "woes." When the Pharisee who invited Jesus to dine with him notes that Jesus did not observe the ritual washing before the meal, this Pharisee becomes amazed at the oversight. Jesus laments at the attitudes of the Pharisees who clean the outside of the cup and the dish by following the prescripts of the Law while the inside of the cup is filled with evil. Jesus invites them to give alms as a means of cleaning the inside of the cup. Jesus' first "woe" laments the Pharisees' practice of making laws for minor details and neglecting the major demands of the Law, such as justice and love of God. Jesus calls them to practice the great and small demands of the Law. In his second "woe," he is saddened by the Pharisees' practice of seeking the places of honor in synagogues and in the marketplaces. The last "woe" warns against being as hidden tombs that internally hide their decay while looking very ordinary on the outside.

A lawyer foolishly rebukes Jesus for seeming to include scholars of the Law in his critique of the Pharisees. Jesus turns on the scholars with three "woes," many of whom belonged to the Pharisee group, though some did not. In his first "woe," Jesus challenges those who place heavy burdens on the people by their interpretation of the Law but do nothing to make the Law livable. In his second "woe," he questions the practice of the scholars who build tombs for the prophets murdered by their ancestors in an attempt to lessen their own guilt, yet they are rejecting Jesus—the greatest of the prophets. God knew the prophets would be killed, but the present generation now becomes responsible for the blood of those killed for God—from Abel to Zechariah (the first and last recorded martyrs in the Old Testament)—as Jesus is the greatest of prophets.

Jesus' final woe is cast upon lawyers who call themselves interpreters of the Law but who truly do not know how to interpret it. When Jesus leaves them, the scribes and Pharisees show open hostility toward the Lord, posing many questions in an attempt to trick him into saying something to condemn himself.

12:1–12 Trusting and witnessing to Jesus

Luke continues to write about the large number of people who follow Jesus when he describes the crowd as being so large that the people were trampling one another. He places together several sayings of Jesus that are also found in the Gospel of Matthew but not linked together in the same order found in Luke. Jesus warns his disciples against the yeast (influence) of the Pharisees. This yeast, which affects the whole loaf, is hypocrisy. In time, all hypocrisy will be recognized as such and cease to be, for nothing can be hidden from God. All spoken in darkness will be known in the light of day, and the words spoken behind locked doors will be heard as if shouted from the rooftops.

Jesus addresses his disciples as "my friends" and urges them not to fear those who can bring only physical death, but rather to fear God, who can bring eternal destruction. Jesus points out the concern God has for sparrows, a common and inexpensive bird used by the poor in Temple sacrifice. And human beings are far more important to God, for even the number of hairs on our heads are counted. The message is that God is greatly concerned for our well-being and that we have nothing to fear.

Those willing to witness to Jesus in the world will have the glorified Christ (the Son of Man) witness for them in heaven; thus, the reverse is also true. Those who speak against the message and person of Christ (the Son of Man) have a chance for forgiveness, while those who refuse to listen to the message deriving from the Holy Spirit have chosen to cut themselves off from the Word of God. Because they have chosen to close their ears totally to God's Word, God is not able to forgive them. Jesus urges his disciples not to worry about how or what they will say in the midst of persecution, because the Holy Spirit will guide them as they witness.

Review Questions

1. Does Jesus really answer prayer when we pray with persistence?
2. Why do the people accuse Jesus of casting out demons by the power of Beelzebul?
3. Why do we have to remain spiritually alert, even after turning from sin and dedicating our lives to God?
4. How strong is our belief that God will take care of us when we are rejected, insulted, or even worse for our faith? Where have we witnessed the love of God today?

Closing Prayer (SEE PAGE 14)

Pray the closing prayer now or after *lectio divina*.

Lectio Divina (SEE PAGE 7)

Relax your body and maintain a posture of prayer (back straight, eyes shut, feet flat on the floor). This exercise can take as long as you want, but in the context of this Bible study, 10 to 20 minutes should be sufficient.

The meditations that follow are provided only to help group participants use this prayer form, but note that *lectio* is intended to bring one to a place of prayerful contemplation where the Word of God speaks to the hearer from his or her heart. (See page 7 for further instruction.)

The Lord's Prayer (11:1–13)

When Jesus directs us to ask, seek, or knock, he does not indicate that we should compose a perfect prayer. A wise preacher once said we should offer God our imperfect prayers and cease from praying the "perfect prayer" over and over again, for this prayer will rarely come. The desire to pray is in fact an act of prayer. If our prayer is imperfect, God will answer all the same, delightfully smiling upon us and responding according to God's will.

✠ *What can I learn from this passage?*

Jesus and Beelzebul (11:14–28)

Jealousy and envy can lead to blindness. Jesus casts a demon out of a mute person so that the mute person can speak, but some in the crowd allowed their jealousy of Jesus to blind them from the miraculous in their midst. They accuse Jesus of casting out demons by the power of demons, but it is actually the power of demons that blinds them to Jesus. We can be blinded to goodness around us because of our jealousy, envy, or some other human weakness.

✠ *What can I learn from this passage?*

The demand for a sign (11:29–32)

A woman told a friend that she would open the Bible randomly to find God's will for her, but she never received a solid message from God. The friend told the woman she would find God's will in the Bible, but not in opening it randomly to find the answer. She had to read it carefully and ponder its message.

✠ *What can I learn from this passage?*

Live in the light (11:33–54)

The Pharisees speak and act as though they are holy and fulfilling the Law, but they are only seeking the approval of others by appearing to be something they are not. Jesus seeks spiritually mature people who not only speak God's Word but also live God's Word.

✠ *What can I learn from this passage?*

Trusting and witnessing to Jesus (12:1–12)

When a high school student refused to play a football game because it was scheduled on a Sunday morning when he ordinarily would be at worship, the coach and others tried to persuade the boy to play in this important game. The boy refused and was ridiculed by his classmates, but still he remained firm. Very few of us will be martyrs for the faith, but there are times when we must stand firm and perhaps face ridicule and rejection among those close to us for our decision to remain faithful to our call as a Christian.

✠ *What can I learn from this passage?*

PART 2: INDIVIDUAL STUDY (LUKE 12:13—13:7)

Day 1: The Parable of the Rich Fool (12:13–21)

A voice from the crowd cries out to Jesus to solve a dispute between him and his brother over an inheritance. Jesus, whose mission is to teach a religious message, points out that he does not arbitrate in cases such as this except to warn against the sinfulness of those filled with human greed.

Jesus relates a parable about a rich man who had an abundant harvest and who, using his worldly wisdom, decides to tear down his barns and build larger ones to store his abundant crop of grain. When he has enough security to provide for his needs for many years, he is ready to enjoy a life of relaxation and wealth. What he could not control was the length of his own life, and God, who will demand the man's life that very night, calls him a fool because he did not prepare for eternal life. When the man dies, his riches go to someone else, and he finds he has no riches in matters pertaining to God. Through this parable, Jesus is indirectly responding to the man who is having a dispute with his brother concerning the inheritance.

Lectio Divina

Spend 8 to 10 minutes in silent contemplation of the following passage:

> Some build their hope, power, and prestige on wealth, while others build their life on generously sharing whatever talents they have with those in need. Jesus calls the man who allows his wealth to become the driving force in his life a fool. We will all die. The fool has nothing left when he or she is called from this life, but the generous person is promised eternal life with Jesus.

✠ *What can I learn from this passage?*

Day 2: Depending on God (12:22–34)

Jesus uses the parable of the rich fool as the foundation of his teaching about trust in God. He reminds his listeners that they are concerned about the food they eat and the clothing they wear instead of the manner in which they live. Because God cares so well for the birds of the air who do not store up wealth for themselves, then the people, who are far more important, should realize that God also cares for them.

Human beings cannot match the splendor God has given to the world. Through God's providence, the flowers grow without toiling or spinning, yet not even King Solomon, with all his riches and glory, could equal the magnificence of the flowers of the field. Solomon was the richest and most luxuriant of all the kings of Israel. If God shows such care for the grass that has only a passing beauty and use, how much more will God show concern for his human creation, destined for eternal life? Jesus addresses his audience as people of little faith, since so many worldly concerns weight them down.

Jesus tells his audience not to worry about what they are to eat and drink. The pagans of the world make the things of the world their primary concern. Those who have faith believe that God will provide, and they make the kingdom of God their first aim, trusting God to provide the rest. Because the followers of Jesus have chosen the kingdom of God, they should be willing to cast aside their worldly concerns for the sake of helping others. Jesus urges them to sell their belongings and give alms, and to be faithful; making the kingdom of God their true treasure, a treasure which no one can take from them and stored up for all eternity. Whatever

---

a person chooses as most important in life, the individual's heart will seek the path that leads to that treasure.

Lectio Divina

Spend 8 to 10 minutes in silent contemplation of the following passage:

Jesus urges us to pray, but as humans, we often expect immediate results as God is now obliged to answer our prayer. When we pray, however, we are speaking to God, who has a greater love for us than he does for the birds of the air and the flowers of the field. Even when we do not perceive an answer to our prayer, we can conclude that God is acting in some fashion.

✠ *What can I learn from this passage?*

Day 3: The Vigilant and Faithful Servants (12:35–48)

Jesus relates a parable concerning the need to be prepared for the master's return from a wedding, that is, the coming of the Son of Man at the end of time. Wedding celebrations in Jesus' era could continue for days, and the servants were never sure when their master would return. During the absence of the master, the doors would be locked until the master came and knocked on the door. The faithful servants are those who are ready to open when the master knocks. True servants show their readiness with their belts fastened around their waists and their lamps burning, ready to serve the master.

Jesus states that the master who finds his servants prepared for his return will put on an apron and wait on those he finds awake upon his return. As unlikely as such an action sounds, it does reflect the manner in which the Son of Man will treat those whom he finds faithful (awake) when he comes again. As he has done throughout his ministry, Jesus willingly serves them because they have served him. If the master in the parable delays his arrival and still finds his servants prepared for his return, he will reward them. Just as someone would be prepared if he or she knew when a thief intended to break into the house, so the disciples of Jesus should be prepared for the return of the Son of Man at the least expected time.

Peter, serving as a representative of the early Church, asks Jesus if he intends the parable for them alone or for everyone. In his response to the question, Jesus speaks of "the prudent steward" who waits for his master's return. This was an exhortation for the early Church to share their gifts with one another and await the return of Jesus. If the members of the early Church perform their function well, Jesus will entrust them with even more when the end comes. If the members of the early Church do not perform their duties well but abuse others, then the master will come unexpectedly and deprive those servants of the gifts placed in their trust. Those who knowingly misuse the gifts given to them by the master (Jesus) will receive a severe punishment, while those who unknowingly misuse these gifts will receive a light punishment. Jesus declares that much will be required of the one entrusted with much, and more will be required of the person who has received even more.

Lectio Divina

Spend 8 to 10 minutes in silent contemplation of the following passage:

> Followers of Jesus cannot live their lives thinking only of their own needs, but they must think like stewards in a household, sharing God's gifts with others and being ready when God, the master, calls us. Jesus adds a strange note to his message, saying that the master will have the servants recline at table and wait on them, serving the needs of those who remain faithful.

✠ *What can I learn from this passage?*

Day 4: The Effects of Jesus' Message (12:49–59)

Jesus has come to spread his message across the land like fire. The symbol of fire refers to the gift of the Holy Spirit that Jesus wishes to give the world. Jesus speaks of the great pain and anguish he feels at his own "baptism," that is, his passion, death, and resurrection. Jesus did not come to share a peace that leaves everyone living in tranquility. On the contrary, family members will be divided among themselves over the message of Jesus. When Luke was writing his gospel, many families rejected their sons, daughters, fathers, mothers, or in-laws because they chose to profess faith in Jesus Christ.

Luke adds another of Jesus' sayings when he speaks of Jesus as challenging the people to recognize the signs of the times, namely, that the reign of God is at hand. Just as the people can read the changes in weather by the clouds and the wind, so they should learn to read the spiritual changes taking place at the coming of Jesus. Jesus calls them hypocrites because they have worldly wisdom but lack spiritual wisdom.

No one needs to have any special wisdom to realize that a settlement must be made with an opponent before the case reaches the magistrate and a person ends up in jail. The punishment will last until the person pays the last penny.

Lectio Divina

Spend 8 to 10 minutes in silent contemplation of the following passage:

No matter how intelligent it may sound for some to reject God because they do not see God's face, Christians believe that truth is not always visible to the human eye. Truth often relies on faith in Jesus' message. Christians have learned to read the signs of the times, which is a time to recognize that Jesus has come and has left us with a message of love.

✠ *What can I learn from this passage?*

Day 5: Warning About Judgment (13:1–9)

Two incidents, apparently well known to the people of Jesus' day, prompt Jesus to warn about the Final Judgment. Pilate had his men slaughter some Galileans who offered sacrifices in the Temple. The people tell Jesus about this event, and also the event in which a tower at Siloam collapsed and killed eighteen people. The people imply that these events showed God's judgment upon those people. Jesus replies that God does not act in this way, but he warns his listeners that their lives will end as suddenly as those Pilate slaughtered and those who were killed by the collapse of the tower at Siloam.

Jesus tells the story of the barren fig tree, which is used in the Old Testament as a symbol of Israel. When the owner comes to gather fruit from the tree, he finds none and orders the gardener to cut the tree down.

The gardener begs the owner to leave the tree alone for another year and allow him to fertilize and care for it. If it does not bear fruit in that time, then the owner can have it cut down. The story reflects God's desire for all to be saved, even to the point of extending one's life for the sake of salvation. In his case, Jesus is saying that God is not anxious to reject Israel, but is willing to allow the people of Judea more time to recognize Jesus as the Christ.

Lectio Divina

Spend 8 to 10 minutes in silent contemplation of the following passage:

Like the gardener who wants the owner to give the fig tree more time to produce fruit and promises to work more vigorously on the soil, Jesus is telling us that God gives us more time to repent and showers more graces on us. Unfortunately, not all respond to these gifts from God.

✠ *What can I learn from this passage?*

Day 6: Jesus Heals a Crippled Woman (13:10–17)

The barrenness of Israel is further illustrated by an incident in a synagogue on the Sabbath. A woman who was bent over and crippled for eighteen years calls out to Jesus. Jesus heals the woman by placing his hand on her, enabling her to stand erect. The leader of the synagogue becomes upset with the healing, fearing that the Sabbath rest would be interrupted by people seeking cures. He speaks on behalf of other opponents of Jesus when he reminds the people that they have six days to work and seek cures but that they should not seek them on the Sabbath. Jesus addresses the leader and his other opponents as hypocrites because they dare to lead their animals to water on the Sabbath, but they do not allow a descendant of Abraham, who was afflicted for eighteen years, to be healed on the Sabbath. The opponents of Jesus are shamed by his answer, but the crowds rejoice "at all the splendid deeds done by him."

Lectio Divina

Spend 8 to 10 minutes in silent contemplation of the following passage:

> For many people, the Lord's Day has become a time for doing good, namely, worshiping, visiting the homebound or people in nursing homes or hospitals, helping neighbors in need, spending time with the family, and speaking words of encouragement to those suffering from grief or despair. Performing good deeds on the day of rest is a perfect way to celebrate the Lord's Day.

✠ *What can I learn from this passage?*

Review Questions

1. How are we challenged to trust in God?

2. How could living our faith in today's world be a cause for division? Think of some examples.

3. What lesson do we take away from the parable of the fig tree?

4. Name or list some good deeds that could be performed on the Lord's Day.

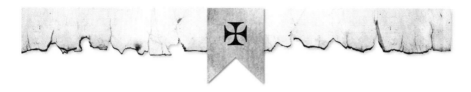

God's Joy Over Repentant Sinners

LUKE 13:18—17:19

While he [the prodigal son] was still a long way off, his father caught sight of him, and was filled with compassion. He ran to his son, embraced him and kissed him (15:20).

Opening Prayer (SEE PAGE 14)

Context

Part 1: Luke 13:18—15:32 Jesus delivers parables about a mustard seed and yeast as a symbol of the kingdom of God. He speaks of the narrow door leading to God's reign, heals a man with dropsy, delivers parables about banquets, and calls his disciples to pick up their cross and follow him. He presents three parables to show how important the sinner is to God.

Part 2: Luke 16:1—17:19 Jesus delivers a parable about an unjust steward, which is followed by a series of sayings against the Pharisees, the importance of the Law, and a message about divorce. He relates another parable to warn against ignoring those in need, and he teaches about the dangers of setting a bad example to a new convert and teaches a need for faith. Disciples must be servants to others. Jesus cleanses ten people with leprosy, but only one returns to thank him.

PART 1: GROUP STUDY (LUKE 13:18—15:32)

Read aloud Luke 13:18—15:32.

13:18–21 Parables of the mustard seed and yeast

Jesus presents two parables that speak of humble beginnings, intended to lead to something greater. In the story of the mustard seed, the seed becomes a great bush and offers protection to the birds of the air. The mustard seed represents the reign of God, growing abundantly. The image of the birds of the air that dwell in the bush refers to the many people throughout the ages who will find a dwelling place in God's reign.

In a second parable, Jesus speaks of the bit of yeast that affects a large amount of wheat. This small amount leavens the whole batch of wheat. Jesus alludes to the insignificant beginnings of the kingdom of God, which eventually becomes great and influential in creation.

13:22–35 The narrow door

Jesus travels through the towns and cities, teaching the people and heading for the holy city of Jerusalem. When someone asks him if only a few will be saved, Jesus does not answer the question directly, but he warns that the way to salvation is through a narrow door. The close followers of Jesus enter this narrow door, while many others will strive to enter through the narrow door but will not be able to do so. The door is finally closed as Jesus tells of the master of a house locking the door to those outside. Many cry out that they knew Jesus, but knowing Jesus is not enough. In the parable, the master will claim that he does not know those outside, though they will recall eating and drinking with him and listening to his speech in their neighborhoods. Because they never accepted the message of the master (Jesus) and did not become his true followers, he will have to say that he does not know them. Addressing them as evildoers because they rejected him, they are cast out.

The message seems to point also to the Israelite nation, who knew Jesus as a member of their nation but rejected his invitation to accept faith in him. Now as they stand outside, they will see the fathers of the Israelite nation (Abraham, Isaac, and Jacob), along with all the prophets, sharing in the banquet of the kingdom of God. They will also see strangers (Gentiles) from every end of the Earth sharing in the banquet. The Israelites, who knew God's promise of salvation, were chosen to be first in the kingdom, but now the Gentiles, who learned of God's promise of salvation last, were chosen to become first in the kingdom of God. The message refers not only to the Israelite nation but also to the people of the early Church. Those who were first invited to be heirs of the reign of God can lose it through their own fault, while those who come to knowledge of the kingdom later in life can become first in the kingdom. The quality of dedication is more important than the time of dedication.

Some Pharisees come to Jesus to warn him that Herod has plans to kill him. Jesus calls Herod a fox, apparently in reference to his effort to try to trap Jesus. Jesus declares that human forces do not have the power to decide his fate. He will continue to cast out devils and healing until his allotted time, when he shall die like the prophets of old, in the holy city of Jerusalem. Jesus tells them that his purpose will be accomplished on the third day, an apparent reference to the day of his resurrection.

At the mention of Jerusalem, Jesus turns his attention to that city and laments over it. Jesus wanted to care for his city like a mother hen protecting her young under her wing. But the people of Jerusalem continue to kill the prophets and those sent to preach to them. Jesus states that their house will be abandoned. This is a reference to the Temple of Jerusalem that will be abandoned, a prediction that implies that the religious center of the city will die. The next time they see Jesus, they will truly recognize him and praise him as the one who comes in the name of the Lord. This is a reference to Jesus' triumphant entry into Jerusalem.

14:1–24 Jesus dines and teaches

Jesus dines at the home of a leading Pharisee on the Sabbath, and Luke uses this occasion for Jesus to teach lessons about the Sabbath, about seeking the highest place at table, and about accepting an invitation to the banquet of the Lord. The first event deals with healing on the Sabbath, a theme Luke treated earlier in his gospel (13:10–17) concerning the curing of a crippled woman on the Sabbath. A man with dropsy is in front of Jesus, which means he was most likely one of the guests. Dropsy is a bloating of the body due to an abnormal retention of fluid. Jesus asks the scholars of the Law and the Pharisees if it is lawful to heal on the Sabbath. The leaders remain silent, and Jesus heals the man and dismisses him. Jesus confronts them with their own actions on the Sabbath. Would they have a son or an ox fall into a pit on the Sabbath and not rescue either one? Luke tells us they could not answer the question, most likely because they saw the logic of healing versus rescuing a son or ox from a cistern.

During the meal, Jesus uses an image from worldly glory to stress a point in a parable concerning the place of honor at table. He tells his listeners that they should not seek the places of honor at table, lest they be humiliated by being asked to take a lower place when a more honored guest arrives. Rather, they should take a lower place so that the host, in front of all the guests, might invite them to a higher place. Although the motive for taking the lower place seems to be earthly glory in being honored by the host, Jesus applies this to the spiritual life of his followers, declaring that those who humble themselves will be exalted, and those who exalt themselves will be humbled.

Jesus often plays down one point to stress another. As he continues to share his message at the home of the Pharisee, Jesus tells his listeners that they should not invite their friends, relatives, or wealthy neighbors to the banquet so that they will return the invitation. They should invite the poor, the sick, and the outcasts who cannot reciprocate. Jesus does not intend to teach that one should ignore friends, relatives, or neighbors who happen to have wealth, but he intends to challenge the motive for invitations to gatherings. The poor and the outcast can certainly make no returns, and the only return that will be made is at the resurrection of the just.

As the dinner continues, Jesus shares another parable. The mention of resurrection turns the thoughts of one of the listeners to the kingdom of God, and he responds to Jesus' words with an expression of blessing for those who will dine in the kingdom of God. Jesus uses this mention of the kingdom of God as the occasion to relate another parable. The image of the kingdom of God as a banquet is used often in the Old Testament, and Jesus uses this image in his story.

Jesus tells of a man who sends his servant out to his invited guests to tell them the banquet is ready, but those invited begin to excuse themselves, using such excuses as the purchase of a field, the purchase of five yoke of oxen, or a recent marriage. The invited guests are the people of Israel who treat the invitation as secondary to their daily lives. When the servants return with the excuses, the angry host then sends out his servants to the streets and alleys to bring in those who are poor, diseased, crippled, and other outcasts. Even after the outcasts come, there is still room, and now the host tells the servants to go out and make others come in. Jesus ends his parable by stating that none of those invited will taste the dinner.

The banquet parable refers first to the Israelites, who are the Chosen People, the invited guests, but they refuse to accept Jesus' invitation. The outcasts refer to those in Jewish society who are often seen as sinners or those rejected by God. They accept the invitation to the banquet, the reign of God. Those from the highways refer to the Gentiles, who were not originally invited to the feast, but this parable extends the invitation for all to accept God's reign. In the story, the host declares that those first invited (the self-righteous among the Israelites) shall not take part in the banquet of the Lord.

14:25–35 The cost of discipleship

Luke continues to speak about the great crowds following Jesus. Jesus addresses the crowds with shocking words about the need to hate one's father, mother, wife, children, brothers, sisters, and even one's own life to become his disciple. Jesus is declaring that the call to be a follower of Jesus is a radical call, one that is so strong the disciples must be willing to follow Jesus despite family ties and even their own will. When Jesus speaks of "hating" one's family, he means the true disciple must be willing to follow Christ, no matter what the cost. The word *hate* in this passage does not refer to showing a lack of love for another; it means a disciple must be willing to suffer rejection from close relatives rather than deny Christ. A disciple must be willing to take up the cross, a symbol of suffering and mockery. At the time Luke is writing about this willingness to take up one's cross, he is already familiar with the crucifixion of Jesus and Jesus' resurrection. If Jesus used the term during his lifetime, no one would have understood the impact of its meaning. Jesus most likely called for sacrifice on the part of his disciples, but he would have used a different image for his message.

In two short parables, Jesus tells his listeners that they should not make this commitment to sacrifice oneself for him lightly, but should determine whether they have the strength to dedicate themselves to true discipleship. Just as a builder of a tower must calculate his materials ahead of time to determine if he has enough to build, and a king must calculate the strength of his own army as he goes out to war against another, so the followers of Jesus must calculate their own depth of commitment to Jesus before accepting the role of discipleship. The disciple must renounce all of one's possessions to follow Jesus.

The disciple filled with such a commitment is one who is like good and useful salt, while the one who does not have the ability to carry out his or her commitment is like bad salt, tasteless and good for nothing. The importance of the message is underlined as Jesus calls those with the ears of faith to hear what he is telling them.

15:1–10 Parables of the lost sheep and coin

The Pharisees complain that Jesus welcomes sinners and eats with them, gestures that seem to imply Jesus is accepting the manner of life of sinners. Jesus uses this occasion to share several parables about the joy of God over one sinner who repents.

Jesus asks who would leave ninety-nine sheep in a field to search after a lost sheep. We can imagine his audience pondering this question and concluding that it would indeed be a bad decision, but Jesus continues with his parable as though they agreed to leave the ninety-nine to go after the lost sheep. He tells of the shepherd's finding the sheep and calling together everyone to share in his joy. Through this story, Jesus expresses God's great love and concern for sinners. Jesus ends his parable by saying there will be more joy in heaven over one sinner who repents than over the ninety-nine who had no need of repentance. In reality, God rejoices as much over those who are not lost as over those who are lost and have returned.

Jesus also tells a parable about a woman who has ten silver coins and loses one. She lights a lamp, sweeps the house, and searches carefully until she finds the lost coin. She then calls her friends and neighbors to celebrate. Jesus says that in the same way, the angels will greatly rejoice over one sinner who repents.

15:11–32 The return of the prodigal son

Here, Jesus narrates a parable of the younger of two sons asking his father for his inheritance, which is akin to asking that he be cut off from the family. The father allows the son to choose his own course in life, even if it means the son will separate himself from the family. Although God loves us, God has given us free will, even though this means we can choose to cut ourselves off from God. The son goes off to squander his inheritance on loose living and eventually loses it all. In a time of famine, the son cares for pigs, the "lowest" animal in Jewish thought. The son has fallen so low that he longs to eat the food given to the pigs, but nobody offers him any. The son decides to return to his father, admit his sin, and ask his father to accept him as a hired hand.

The central message of the story centers on the father, who offers us an image of God. Although the parable says nothing about the grief of the father in granting the younger son's request for his inheritance, it speaks of the father's great love for his son when he catches sight of him in the distance. Moved with compassion, the father runs to his son, embraces him, and kisses him. Without saying it, the father has already expressed his forgiveness of the son. The son, in seeking to work as a hired hand, cannot think in any other way except that of a son. He says, "Father, I have sinned against heaven and against you; I no longer deserve to be called your son." Although he states he is no longer worthy to be called a son, he already betrays his thinking by addressing his father with the term "Father." The father does not rebuke or castigate him; rather, he has the servants put a robe on his son, a ring on his finger, and shoes on his feet. He orders that the servants kill the fatted calf for a celebration, for his son was dead and has now come to life. In clothing his son in a robe, a ring, and shoes, the father (God) is welcoming the son (the sinner) back into the family.

When the elder son learns of the party being given for his brother, he becomes angry and refuses to join in, complaining to the father that he has been a dutiful son with no reward. The older son refuses to speak of the returning son as his brother but speaks to the father about "your son." The father refuses to accept this and refers to the lost son as "your brother" who was dead and has come to life again. The elder son has kept all the

---

rules, but he is not like the father. He does not rejoice over a brother who was dead in sin and has come to life, and unlike the father, he does not forgive his brother or welcome him back into the family.

Review Questions

1. What must we do to enter through the narrow door?
2. How can we apply the message of the banquet stories to our lives?
3. What do the parables of the lost sheep and the lost coin tell us about God?
4. What does the story of the prodigal son reveal to us about God's love and mercy?

Closing Prayer (SEE PAGE 14)

Pray the closing prayer now or after *lectio divina*.

Lectio Divina (SEE PAGE 7)

Relax your body and maintain a posture of prayer (back straight, eyes shut, feet flat on the floor). This exercise can take as long as you want, but in the context of this Bible study, 10 to 20 minutes should be sufficient.

The meditations that follow are provided only to help group participants use this prayer form, but note that *lectio* is intended to bring one to a place of prayerful contemplation where the Word of God speaks to the hearer from his or her heart. (See page 7 for further instruction.)

Parables of the mustard seed and yeast (13:18–21)

Many spectacular growths in the Church began as a tiny seed. One such example is a Catholic fraternal order known as the Knights of Columbus, founded by Father Michael McGivney in 1882. The seed he planted with a small number of people in one parish eventually spread to millions of members throughout the United States. The Knights of Columbus give more than a million dollars to charity each year and donate millions of hours to charitable works. From the growth of the kingdom of God on Earth and the growth of the Knights of Columbus, we learn a lesson about the importance of planting a tiny seed of love and goodness in God's creation.

✠ *What can I learn from this passage?*

The narrow door (13:22–35)

Jesus calls us to love God and our neighbor. This is the narrow door, and it is a challenge for us in our day-to-day life. Faith in God consists not only in words, but also in action.

✠ *What can I learn from this passage?*

Jesus dines and teaches (14:1–24)

Being invited to the banquet means being invited to share in Jesus' life and attitudes. It demands humility by not always seeking the highest spot, but rather by living as a servant as Jesus did. Sharing in the banquet means vesting ourselves in the attitude of love and openness shown by Jesus.

✠ *What can I learn from this passage?*

The cost of discipleship (14:25–35)

We make a new commitment to God with every sacrament we celebrate. If Jesus were living today, he may say to us, "Before you make this commitment, I want you to sit down and seriously consider whether you are able to do this." According to Jesus, we must calculate whether we have enough faith to finish the task or enough spiritual stamina to encounter a strong enemy who challenges our faith.

✠ *What can I learn from this passage?*

Parables of the lost sheep and coin (15:1–10)

After reading Jesus' parables about God's joy over sinners who return, we must wonder how some could feel they have strayed so far from God that they cannot be forgiven. Some of the strongest messages preached by Jesus told of God's great joy over sinners who repent of their sinfulness and are found back in God's good graces.

✠ *What can I learn from this passage?*

The return of the prodigal son (15:11–32)

Many of us run the danger of being more like the elder son who looks down upon the sinner and refuses to see repentance. One of the greatest challenges offered by Christianity is to live up to the creation message, where we are told that we are made in God's image and likeness. We are called to

---

possess the spirit of forgiveness, joy, and love found in the father in this parable. This is a difficult challenge for all Christians.

✠ *What can I learn from this passage?*

PART 2: INDIVIDUAL STUDY (LUKE 16:1—17:19)

Day 1: The Parable of the Dishonest Manager (16:1–18)

Jesus delivers a parable about a steward who mismanaged the master's property. The master calls for an accounting of the steward's management, and the steward, realizing the master will soon dismiss him, looks at his possibilities for the future. He is unable to dig ditches and ashamed to beg, so he decides to place others in his debt with the hope that they will remember his deeds. He reduces each of the debts these people owe by forgoing his commission. A debt of a hundred jars of oil is reduced to fifty, and a debt of a hundred measures of wheat is reduced to eighty. The master, seeing the shrewd decision made by the steward, has to give him credit for his foresight. Those concerned with this world's goods show more dedication than those concerned with the spiritual world.

This parable is difficult to understand, and there have been many different interpretations of it. It seems Jesus is commending the people of the world for using worldly goods for their own selfish ends. The problem with such a commendation is that it does not agree with the total message of Jesus found in the gospels. Jesus himself comments on the parable by telling his listeners to use wisely the world's goods so that, when these goods are no longer useful, they will find a lasting gift awaiting them. The person who uses the gifts of this world wisely will be worthy of the greater gifts of eternal life, because using gifts wisely involves using them as God desires. In using another's wealth (the gifts given by God), true stewards show themselves worthy of receiving these gifts. Jesus ends by declaring that a person cannot serve two masters. The servant must choose either God or money, but not both.

Until the coming of John the Baptist, the Law was in force, but now, with the proclamation of the Good News of the kingdom of God, Jesus offers a new interpretation of the Law and the Prophets. Not only the Israelites, but all people will come into the kingdom, some of them forcefully claiming their right. The Law has not passed away with the coming of Jesus, but true interpretation of the Law is now given by Jesus.

Lectio Divina

Spend 8 to 10 minutes in silent contemplation of the following passage:

> Jesus wisely tells us about the impossibility of serving two masters. If we strive to love Christ and follow his words and example, everything we do will be measured against that attitude. If we strive for worldly rewards like power, prestige, luxury, or pleasure, then everything we do will be measured against this behavior. We choose which master we will follow every day of our lives.

✠ *What can I learn from this passage?*

Day 2: The Rich Man and Lazarus (16:19–31)

Jesus tells about a rich man and a poor beggar named Lazarus, both of whom died. Before their death, the beggar longed for the scraps that fell from the rich man's table, and the rich man ignored this beggar at his gate. In this story, the rich man, who is not named, seems oblivious to the plight of the poor man, whose name is given as Lazarus. The rich man does not simply reject Lazarus; he does not even seem to notice him. In death, Lazarus is brought by angels to Abraham's bosom, that is, the final place of peace for the true descendants of Israel. The rich man dies and is buried. No comment is made about anyone carrying the rich man to his final resting place. The roles are reversed. Lazarus has riches, and the rich man has eternal torture in the flames of Hades. Whereas the beggar once longed for the scraps that fell from the table of the rich man, the rich man now longs for a drop of water from Lazarus.

In the abode of the dead, the rich man and Lazarus see each other, but they cannot cross from one side to the other. When the rich man begs Abraham to send Lazarus to his five brothers to warn them of this fate, Abraham responds that they have Moses and the prophets to direct them. If they do not listen to Moses and the prophets, then they will not listen to someone who rises from the dead. These words are a reference to the resurrection of Jesus. Despite this resurrection, some still will not listen to the message of Jesus.

Lectio Divina

Spend 8 to 10 minutes in silent contemplation of the following passage:

> We know we must reach out to the poor, the homeless, the cold, and all those suffering, but we are often unaware of ways to reach them. We may prefer to look away rather than help. Jesus is telling us that he wants us to become aware of the needs around us and help where we can, even if it means simply supporting those who are dedicated to helping others in need.

✠ *What can I learn from this passage?*

Day 3: The Greatest Commandment (17:1–10)

As Luke portrays Jesus continuing his journey, he links together four sayings of Jesus. In the first saying, Jesus admits that scandal will continually occur, but this does not excuse the person who causes scandal. In Jesus' day, a large millstone turned by beasts of burden was used to grind up wheat. The punishment that awaits the one who causes scandal is so great that it would be better to have such a millstone tied around one's neck and that person be thrown into the sea. Death by drowning was considered a horrible and frightening death for the people of Jesus' day. This first saying of Jesus gives the audience a stern warning against scandal.

In the second saying, Jesus teaches that the one causing scandal should be corrected and forgiven when he or she repents and be forgiven as often as forgiveness is sought. Even if a person wrongs another seven times in one day and seeks forgiveness seven times, the disciple should forgive him or her.

In the third saying, the disciples ask Jesus to increase their faith. Jesus tells them that faith the size of a mustard seed can move something as deeply rooted as a mulberry tree. Since the mustard seed is so small, Jesus could be implying that they have very little faith to begin with.

In the fourth saying, Jesus notes that a master who has a servant coming in from plowing or tending sheep does not invite the servant to take a place at table while the master waits on him. The master would still expect his servant to wait on him and eat and drink later, despite the servant's hard work. The master should not be grateful to the servant because he has done what he was commanded. In the same way, the disciples of Jesus must not believe God is obliged to share gifts with them because they have lived according to the Law. Every gift God gives, whether a person has worked hard or not, comes from the goodness of God and not from any obligation or repayment. Jesus tells us we should recognize with humility that we are humble servants who have done what we are obliged to do.

Lectio Divina

Spend 8 to 10 minutes in silent contemplation of the following passage:

> After living as close to Jesus' Law as we can possibly do, we can only say, "We are unprofitable servants; we have done what we were obliged to do." With this in mind, we live as true servants of Jesus, seeking to serve him without expecting Jesus to feel obliged to reward us. We are, however, grateful that we have a loving God who will reward us.

✠ *What can I learn from this passage?*

Day 4: Jesus Cleanses Ten People With Leprosy (17:11–19)

Jesus continues his journey toward Jerusalem, passing through Samaria and Galilee. Ten people with leprosy, keeping their distance from Jesus as prescribed by the Law, cry out to him for a cure. He does not heal them immediately, but tests their faith by telling them to go and show themselves to the priests, without any sign that they are healed. Luke tells us that the leprosy was healed while they were on their journey. Only one, a Samaritan, returned, praising God in a loud voice. He fell at the feet of Jesus and thanked him, but Jesus questions the absence of the other nine. He says, "Has none but this foreigner returned to give thanks to God?" Jesus dismisses the man, stating that his faith has saved him.

Lectio Divina

Spend 8 to 10 minutes in silent contemplation of the following passage:

In asking the man with leprosy who returned to thank him about the other nine, Jesus is showing God's desire to have us offer thanks for the many gifts granted to us each day. We encounter many of God's blessings at every moment, but we can begin to take them for granted and forget to thank God. Jesus is telling us that God wants to be thanked.

✠ *What can I learn from this passage?*

Review Questions

1. What does the story of the dishonest steward tell us about serving two masters?
2. What lessons can we learn from the rich man and Lazarus?
3. Do we really believe faith can move a mulberry bush?

Jesus' Last Days in Jerusalem

LUKE 17:20—20:19

Blessed is the king who comes in the name of the Lord. Peace in heaven and glory in the highest (19:38).

Opening Prayer (SEE PAGE 14)

Context

Part 1: Luke 17:20—19:10 Jesus warns his listeners not to be deceived when they hear the end is near. He teaches about persistence in prayer and the need for humility. He teaches that the reign of God involves accepting those who are as dependent as little children, and he warns against the difficulties of being rich. After predicting his passion and resurrection a third time, he heals a blind beggar and eats at the house of Zacchaeus, a tax collector.

Part 2: Luke 19:11—20:19 Jesus preaches about the use of God's gifts through a parable about a rich master who gives money to his servants to be used well while he is away. Those who use the gifts well are rewarded, while those who do not use them well lose what they have. Jesus has a triumphal entry into Jerusalem, but he soon laments over the coming destruction of Jerusalem.

PART 1: GROUP STUDY (LUKE 17:20—19:10)

Read aloud Luke 17:20—19:10.

17:20-37 The coming of the kingdom

When the Pharisees ask Jesus when the kingdom of God will come, Jesus warns against calculating the exact time and against following after false prophets. The kingdom of God, he tells them, is already in their midst. Jesus prophesies that his disciples will long to see the day of the Son of Man, but they will not see it, and he warns the disciples against running after false rumors about the return of Christ. The Son of Man will come as suddenly as a flash of lightning. But he must first suffer and be rejected by this generation. The day of the coming of the Son of Man will be no different from any other day. People will be taken up with their daily pursuits, eating, drinking, marrying, buying, selling, building, and planting as they were in the days of Noah and Lot. Jesus is simply saying that the event will catch the people by surprise, not that the world will be sinful as it was when Noah entered the ark.

Jesus then turns his attention to the destruction of Jerusalem as he speaks of those on the housetop at the time the Son of Man is revealed. On the day of the destruction of Jerusalem, Jesus warns, everyone should leave quickly and not turn back.

Jesus returns to the message of the Second Coming when he warns that those who try to preserve their life will lose it, while those who are willing to lose their life will save it. On the day of the Second Coming, one will be taken to glory while the other will be left. Jesus tells them they will know when it takes place, no matter where they are. Just as vultures tell us that one or more carcasses are on the ground, so will we all be aware the Second Coming is taking place.

18:1-8 Parable of the persistent widow

Using a parable, Jesus tells of a widow who harassed a judge who had no regard for God or human beings. She keeps pestering him to the point that he must respond to her request for a just verdict against her adversary. If an unjust judge acts in such a way in the face of persistent requests, how much more readily will God, who loves all, act in the face of persistent requests? Jesus questions whether the Son of Man will find faith on Earth like this woman's when he comes in glory.

18:9–17 Humility and the tax collector

Jesus narrates a parable of a tax collector, who is considered a sinner in the eyes of many of the religious leaders, and a Pharisee, both of whom go to the Temple to pray. The Pharisee is obviously the self-righteous one. He prays boldly, thanks God that he does not have the weakness of others, and especially that he is not like the tax collector. The Pharisee could outshine most people in his religious practice. He practices a strict fast twice a week, and he tithes his riches. These are worthy actions, but his self-righteous spirit ruins it all.

The tax collector, unable to raise his eyes to heaven and beating his breast, expresses his sinfulness a distance from the altar. He begs for God's mercy. Jesus states that in the end, the tax collector goes home justified, while the Pharisee, with all his good works, does not. Jesus continues to challenge the righteousness of the Pharisee, saying that those who exalt themselves will be humbled and those who humble themselves will be exalted.

Jesus' disciples try to discourage the people from bringing their children to Jesus, but Jesus directs his disciples not to hinder them, declaring that the kingdom of God belongs to the little ones. Jesus uses them as an example of trust, implying that those with the spirit of children already share in the kingdom of God.

18:18–30 The rich man and Jesus

One of the religious leaders approaches Jesus to ask what he must do to gain everlasting life. He calls Jesus "good teacher," and Jesus asks why he calls him "good." In Jewish thought, no one deserves to be called "good" except God. Jesus does not wait for an answer, but tells the rich man to live the commandments. Jesus names five of the commandments, and the rich man responds that he has lived up to them. Jesus gives him a last command, to give up all he has, give it to the poor, and follow him. This will ensure that he will have a treasure in heaven. The rich man, unfortunately, cannot bring himself to part with his wealth.

Jesus expresses how difficult it is for the rich to enter the kingdom of God. He uses a Semitic exaggeration, declaring that it is easier for a camel to pass through the eye of a needle (which is impossible) than for someone who is rich to enter heaven. With God, however, the impossible becomes possible, and the rich will be able to enter the kingdom of God. Peter asks what those who have left everything for the sake of the kingdom of God can expect in return. Jesus responds that those who have left their home and relatives for the sake of the kingdom of God will receive much in this age and in the one to come, namely, everlasting life.

18:31–43 Understanding Jesus

For the third time, Jesus predicts his passion, death, and resurrection. As he nears Jerusalem, the details become more explicit. Jesus will fulfill the words of the prophets concerning the Son of Man. In this case, Son of Man refers to the suffering servant prophesied in the Book of Isaiah. Jesus predicts his betrayal into the hands of the Gentiles (Romans) and his trial, scourging, death, and resurrection on the third day. The Twelve still do not understand Jesus' words.

As Jesus was approaching Jericho, a blind man, hearing a crowd passing by, asks what is happening. When he hears that Jesus of Nazareth is passing by, he calls out to him by his messianic title, "Son of David." The disciples try to silence the man, but he calls out even louder for Jesus, the Son of David, to have pity on him. Jesus orders the man be brought to him, and he makes the man explicitly ask for his sight. Jesus declares that he is healed because of his faith. The placement of the story of the blind man at this point is a reminder of the blindness of the disciples who do not understand what Jesus is teaching them. Eventually, they will be able to see with the eyes of faith.

19:1–10 Zacchaeus the tax collector

Zacchaeus is a small man and a rich tax collector who has to climb a tree to see Jesus. Jesus invites himself to Zacchaeus's home to dine with the tax collector, whom the people view as a sinner. Zacchaeus responds with an immediate conversion. He addresses Jesus with the title "Lord," and promises to give half of all he has to the poor. He declares that he will make amends with those he cheated by giving them back four times the amount he took from them. Others begin to murmur about Jesus going to the home of a sinner. Despite the murmuring, Jesus declares that Zacchaeus, as a descendant of Abraham, has a right to this call to salvation that he has accepted. The mission of Jesus, the Son of Man (the Messiah), is to save those who are lost.

Review Questions

1. What does the parable of the persistent widow teach us?
2. Why is the prayer of the tax collector more acceptable to God than the prayer of the dutiful Pharisee?
3. What can we learn from the story of the blind beggar calling out to Jesus?
4. What is significant about the story of Zacchaeus?

Closing Prayer (SEE PAGE 14)

Pray the closing prayer now or after *lectio divina*.

Lectio Divina (SEE PAGE 7)

Relax your body and maintain a posture of prayer (back straight, eyes shut, feet flat on the floor). This exercise can take as long as you want, but in the context of this Bible study, 10 to 20 minutes should be sufficient.

The meditations that follow are provided only to help group participants use this prayer form, but note that *lectio* is intended to bring one to a place of prayerful contemplation where the Word of God speaks to the hearer from his or her heart. (See page 7 for further instruction.)

The coming of the kingdom (17:20–37)

The man asked his friend, "What would you do if you knew this was going to be the last day of your life?" The friend answered that he would do what he did every day of his life, namely, eat breakfast, pray for half an hour, go off to work, return home in the evening, pray a little, read the paper, eat, watch television, and go to bed. Although he was not anxious for his life to end, he was ready when God called him.

✠ *What can I learn from this passage?*

Parable of the persistent widow (18:1–8)

A woman, who wanted to know how desperately her little girl wanted a doll, kept telling her daughter she would think about it. When the daughter stopped asking, the mother said, "Don't stop pestering me." In the same way, we keep on pestering God with our prayers, knowing that God is somehow answering our prayers. Jesus is telling us in the gospels, "Don't stop pestering me."

✠ *What can I learn from this passage?*

Humility and the tax collector (18:9–17)

When we do something well, we must realize that God gave us the talent and the opportunity to perform that good deed. Jesus reminds us that we are God's children who, like children, are not always without some fault. Therefore, as children and servants of God, we can do nothing else except to act with humility, realizing that all the good we do, we do in service to God and neighbor, with the help of God.

✠ *What can I learn from this passage?*

The rich man and Jesus (18:18–30)

Jesus does not condemn wealth, but he notes the difficulties attached to it. Many rich people donate a great deal to charity. Others, however, choose to gain wealth for the sake of wealth alone. Some chose to give up everything to follow Christ. Offering oneself to share with others can bring a different and more lasting kind of wealth.

✠ *What can I learn from this passage?*

Understanding Jesus (18:31–43)

When Jesus asks a blind man what he wants, the blind man begs, "Lord, please let me see." This play on words could actually be a prayer for greater insight, that is, for a greater gift of faith rather than the ability to see with the eyes. Although we believe Jesus is the Christ and the Son of God, we too may have a need for a greater faith to make this belief a driving force in our life. We pray, "Lord, please let me see with the eyes of faith."

✠ *What can I learn from this passage?*

Zacchaeus the tax collector (19:1–10)

Jesus invites himself into our lives as he did with Zacchaeus, but he never forces us to respond. That depends on our free will. When Zacchaeus went to his post that day, he had no idea that his life would be completely different by nightfall. A response to Jesus' invitation in our life could change us in an instant.

✠ *What can I learn from this passage?*

PART 2: INDIVIDUAL STUDY (LUKE 19:11—20:19)

Day 1: Parable of the Demanding Nobleman (19:11–27)

Luke links two parables together to form a single story. In the first parable, Jesus tells of a nobleman going to a distant country to become a king. He leaves money with ten of his servants, telling them to trade with the money until he returns. Luke adds the second parable at this point when he mentions that some citizens sent a delegation to the higher rulers, asking that they not make this nobleman a king. When the ruler returns crowned as a king, Luke returns to the first story.

The king calls those servants to whom he gave the money to learn what profit they had earned in trading. Two of the servants bring a profit to the king, which is double the amount he gave them, while a third returns exactly with what he received, expressing his fear of investing and losing the money. The ones who have gained more are given positions of rank in the kingdom, while the one who gained nothing loses what he has, and it is given to another. The third servant's own words condemn him. The king states that the man knew the king was demanding, and he should have acted on this belief. God is a demanding God when it comes to the use of the gifts we have received.

Luke returns to the second parable. The king orders those who tried to stop him from becoming king to be slain in his presence. In 4 BC, Archelaeus went to Rome to be crowned king after the death of his father, Herod the Great. Although he was crowned king, a delegation succeeded in restricting his power to a smaller area than Archelaeus had hoped to receive.

When he returned as king, he had those who tried to stop his crowning slaughtered. Luke seems to be alluding to this event in the second parable woven into this passage.

Lectio Divina

Spend 8 to 10 minutes in silent contemplation of the following passage:

> Jesus told the parable of the nobleman who left his wealth with his servants to remind us that God left the development of creation in our hands. We are co-creators with God. Some of us will use our gifts well and receive a reward when the king (God) returns for us, and others will either hide their gifts or misuse them and find that the gifts will be taken from them when the king returns. With our free will, we accept the gifts and make the decision as to how we will use them.

✠ *What can I learn from this passage?*

Day 2: Triumph and Lament in Jerusalem (19:28–44)

The second part of Luke's Gospel is structured around Jesus' journey to Jerusalem and the events that take place in this city. Jesus' actions challenge the authority of the religious leaders in Jerusalem, leading to his passion, death, and resurrection.

The people of the Old Testament expected the Messiah to come to them from the Mount of Olives, and Jesus does just that. The prophet Zechariah adds, "Exult greatly, O daughter Zion! Shout for joy, O daughter Jerusalem! Behold: your king is coming to you, a just savior is he, humble and riding on a donkey, on a colt, the foal of a donkey" (9:9). Jesus sends two of his disciples ahead with directions to find a colt upon which no one has yet ridden. Riding on a colt shows that he comes in humility and peace, not in military triumph. It also points to the sacredness of Jesus, as he chooses an animal that has not yet been put to any profane use. If anyone asks the disciples the reason for taking the beast, they are to say, "The Master has need of it." When the disciples explain to the owner of the colt that Jesus has need of the animal, he allows the disciples to take it.

The disciples treat Jesus as royalty, spreading their cloaks on the animal before Jesus mounts and laying their cloaks on the ground before him as he enters Jerusalem. Luke follows Mark closely here and gives no motive for the crowds acting in such a manner at this time. Luke alone adds the reaction of the Pharisees, who try to order Jesus to silence his disciples. Jesus declares that even if the disciples were silenced, the stones of the city would call out in praise of Jesus.

The mood changes swiftly as Jesus weeps over the people of Jerusalem. They do not understand God's plan for them, and they will face destruction because of this lack of understanding. Jesus makes a reference to the invasion of Jerusalem by the Romans in the year 70, when the enemy armies would surround the city, killing and maiming many of the inhabitants and destroying the city to the point that there will not remain one stone upon another.

Lectio Divina

Spend 8 to 10 minutes in silent contemplation of the following passage:

Someone once said that God often gives us our Palm Sundays before our Good Fridays. We can often experience the presence of God in our lives before we enter a dry period in prayer or before some tragedy strikes to challenge our faith. We all have our struggles in life, but when they occur, we can look back past them to those periods when all was well and know that God, who was with us in good times, will also be with us in difficult times.

✠ *What can I learn from this passage?*

Day 3: Jesus Cleanses the Temple (19:45–20:8)

Luke shortens the account of the cleansing of the Temple as found in the other gospels. He simply mentions that Jesus enters the Temple area and casts out the merchants, claiming as his authority the prophecy of Isaiah (56:7), who declared that the Lord's house is a house of prayer, and the prophecy of Jeremiah (7:11), who proclaimed that the Temple had been taken over by robbers. Despite the anger of the chief priests, the scribes, and the leaders of the people, Jesus continues to teach openly in the Temple. His popularity continues to grow among the people, while the chief priests and the scribes seek a way to destroy him, hesitating to arrest him due to his popularity.

Luke presents the first of four confrontations between Jesus and the religious leaders when a delegation from the Sanhedrin (high priests, Pharisees, and elders) challenges Jesus' authority to cleanse the Temple and teach in the Temple precincts. The Sanhedrin, the highest official body in Judaism, believed they alone had authority over the Temple, a call given to them by God. The question posed by these religious leaders is meant to embarrass Jesus and force him into claiming that his authority comes from God. If Jesus openly states this, then the Sanhedrin could accuse him of blasphemy and arrest him.

Jesus cleverly sidesteps their request by promising to answer their question if they would first answer his question. He asks them whether the authority of the baptism of John the Baptist came from heaven or was of human origin. The Sanhedrin cannot answer Jesus without condemning themselves. If they say it came from God, the people could rightly ask why they did not accept John's baptism; and if they deny that it came from God, they could face death by stoning at the hands of a crowd that believed John was a prophet. Jesus knows if they do not understand the source of John's authority, they cannot know the source of his authority. When the members of the Sanhedrin claim ignorance about John's authority, Jesus refuses to tell them the source of his authority.

Lectio Divina

Spend 8 to 10 minutes in silent contemplation of the following passage:

Faith changes our attitude toward the world and our attitude toward the Bible. For those who do not believe in Jesus, the New Testament is a mere literary book, while for believers, it offers insight into the Son of God and our call as followers of Jesus.

✠ *What can I learn from this passage?*

Day 4: Parable of the Rebellious Tenants (20:9–19)

Jesus begins his second confrontation with the scribes and chief priests when he narrates a parable about a farmer who sublets his vineyard to tenant farmers while he goes on a journey. In the Old Testament, the image of a vineyard is used to symbolize Israel (Isaiah 5:1–7). The tenants in Jesus' parable are the religious leaders who beat the servants (the prophets sent by God) who were sent to collect the owner's share of the crop.

The owner finally decides to send his son, a reference for Jesus, but the tenants drag him outside the vineyard and kill him. In the Gospel of Luke, like that of Matthew, the son in the story is dragged outside the vineyard, just as Jesus is dragged outside of Jerusalem to be killed. Jesus asks the crowd what the owner would do to the tenant farmers, and the answer is obvious; he will put the tenants to death and give the vineyard to other tenants. The people realize that Jesus is applying the parable to them. They exclaim, "Let it not be so!"

Jesus quotes from Psalm 118:22, declaring that the stone rejected by the builders will become the cornerstone of the structure. Those who destroy that stone (Jesus) will be crushed, referencing the religious leaders who reject Jesus. Those who accept Jesus' message (the disciples of Jesus) will find that the stone will become the cornerstone of the new Israel. The religious leaders, recognizing themselves in the story, become even more eager to seize Jesus immediately, but they fear the reaction of the crowd and must wait for another opportunity.

Lectio Divina

Spend 8 to 10 minutes in silent contemplation of the following passage:

> We may feel that God has chosen us to pass on his message, but we are still tenant farmers in God's creation who could attempt to kill or reject the prophets in our midst. We have a gift from God, and we must pass on that gift to others. Christians have the duty of sharing the fruits of the vineyard with the master of the vineyard (God) and with those who are meant to profit from the vineyard (the human family).

✠ *What can I learn from this passage?*

Review Questions

1. What responsibilities do we have concerning the gifts God has given us?

2. Why did the people receive Jesus with such praise as he entered Jerusalem?

3. What is the meaning of the parable of the tenant farmers and how can it be a warning to Christians?

Jesus Offers His Body and Blood

LUKE 20:20—22:53

He said to them, "I have eagerly desired to eat this Passover with you before I suffer, for, I tell you, I shall not eat it [again] until there is fulfillment in the kingdom of God" (22:15–16).

Opening Prayer (SEE PAGE 14)

Context

Part 1: Luke 20:20—21:19 The leaders challenge Jesus with questions about paying taxes to Caesar and the reality of resurrection. Jesus praises a widow who gives out of her need to the Temple treasury, and he follows this with a prediction about the destruction of the Temple, the sign of the end times, and the persecution the disciples will first have to suffer.

Part 2: Luke 21:20—22:53 Jesus speaks about a time of destruction for Jerusalem and the coming of the Son of Man. He warns his disciples to be vigilant. In the Passion narrative, Luke begins with the conspiracy against Jesus, followed by the Last Supper. Judas betrays Jesus, and Jesus predicts that Peter will deny him three times. Jesus endures his agony in the garden and is arrested.

PART 1: GROUP STUDY (LUKE 20:20—21:19)

Read aloud Luke 20:20—21:19.

20:20-26 The question of paying taxes

The religious leaders send agents to Jesus. They insincerely praise Jesus as a person who does not fear to proclaim the message of God, no matter what others might think. They then pose a question in an attempt to trap him, believing that no matter how he answers the question, he will condemn himself. When they ask Jesus whether it was permissible to pay tribute to Caesar, they knew that a denial of this duty would openly place Jesus in opposition to Rome, while his acceptance of paying taxes would place him in opposition to many within Judaism.

Jesus, aware of their intention to trap him, asks for a coin and asks whose inscription is on the coin. A denarius was a Roman coin. When they answer that it has the emperor's inscription, Jesus simply states that it then belongs to the emperor. Jesus avoids the trap of the agents of the religious leaders and the ire of the Jewish crowd by telling them they should give to the foreign ruler those things that belong to him and to God the things that belong to God. Jesus' shrewd answer silences the religious leaders' agents.

20:27-40 The issue of resurrection

The Sadducees, a party within Israel who believes the first five books of the Bible (the Torah) are the only true Scriptures, challenge Jesus on the idea of resurrection. Since there is no mention of resurrection in the Torah, the Sadducees, contrary to the belief of the Pharisees, do not believe in resurrection from the dead. They pose a question to Jesus that is based on a law of Moses that prescribes that a man must marry his brother's widow if his brother dies leaving no offspring (Deuteronomy 25:5–6). The Sadducees argue about the absurdity of resurrection when one considers this law given to the people by Moses. If a woman marries seven brothers, all of whom die, the Sadducees ask, whose wife will she be at the time of resurrection?

Jesus answers the Sadducees by pointing out that those who share in the resurrection do not live in the same way as we do on Earth, but they live like the angels. There is no marriage or giving in marriage in the resurrection. Since the Sadducees accepted the Exodus as part of the inspired first five books of the Bible, Jesus chooses an example from the life of Moses in his response. He states that when God appeared to Moses in the burning bush, God told him, "I am...the God of Abraham, the God of Isaac, and the God of Jacob" (Exodus 3:6). This description infers that the patriarchs, though dead to this world, are still alive. God did not say he *was* the God of the patriarchs but that he *is* the God of the patriarchs, which means that Abraham, Isaac, and Jacob still exist in the resurrection. Some of the scribes applaud Jesus' answer.

20:41—21:4 The question about David's son

In this fourth controversy, Jesus poses his own question for the religious leaders. According to Jewish thought, one's ancestor was considered greater than anyone born after him. David, however, in Psalm 110:1, calls his offspring by the title "lord," thus alluding to an offspring greater than himself. The reader of the gospel realizes that Jesus, through his resurrection, has shown himself to be the Lord and Messiah and that he is indeed greater than David. But the people of Jesus' own day could not have understood this. Jesus humiliates the religious leaders who were considered the true interpreters of the Scriptures and who could not answer Jesus' question.

Jesus continues to confront the authority of the scribes by challenging their sinful practices. Jesus warns the people against the external show of the scribes who love to be recognized and treated with great honor yet who rob widows and give the outward appearance of holiness by reciting long prayers. Jesus warns that these men, held in such high religious esteem, will have to face a stern judgment. This did not make Jesus a popular person with them.

Luke follows Mark in presenting a story about a poor widow putting two small coins in the Temple treasury. Jesus declares that this poor widow has given more than the wealthy, because they give out of their surplus, while she gives out of her need, all she has to live on. In Jesus' eyes, she has made the greater contribution since it comes from her very livelihood.

21:5–19 The beginning of the end

The author of the Gospel of Mark appears to know about the Roman threat and destruction of some areas around Jerusalem, but he shows no knowledge of the destruction of Jerusalem. Luke wrote after the destruction. The people of Jesus' age saw the Temple as such a firm structure that no catastrophe, apart from the end of the world, could destroy it. As Jesus' followers admire the rich ornamentation of the Temple, Jesus tells them the day will come when everything will be destroyed. The followers of Jesus believe he is speaking of the end of the world, and they ask when this will happen.

Jesus warns them that many false messiahs will come, passing themselves off as the Christ, and he cautions his followers not to follow these false messiahs. Even when they hear of wars and uprisings, they must not be misled into thinking the end is near. Jesus speaks of great apocalyptic calamities—nation rising against nation, earthquakes, sickness, famine, and great changes in the skies.

Jesus declares that before these catastrophes happen, the disciples must endure persecution in synagogues and prisons, trials before great national leaders—all because of their witness to Christ. Jesus will be with them at this time, giving them wisdom and strength in the face of their oppressors. Their own families will betray them, and some will face death. In the face of this persecution, Jesus urges them to remain firm. In this way, they will save their life; that is, they will reach eternal salvation.

Review Questions

1. Why was Jesus considered shrewd in his answer to the question concerning the paying of taxes to Caesar?
2. How does the belief of the Sadducees concerning resurrection of the dead differ from our belief and why?
3. What does the poor widow's contribution to the Temple tell us?

Closing Prayer (SEE PAGE 14)

Pray the closing prayer now or after *lectio divina.*

Lectio Divina (SEE PAGE 7)

Relax your body and maintain a posture of prayer (back straight, eyes shut, feet flat on the floor). This exercise can take as long as you want, but in the context of this Bible study, 10 to 20 minutes should be sufficient.

The meditations that follow are provided only to help group participants use this prayer form, but note that *lectio* is intended to bring one to a place of prayerful contemplation where the Word of God speaks to the hearer from his or her heart. (See page 7 for further instruction.)

The question of paying taxes (20:20–26)

The image of Caesar here could mean the image of material goods. We are made in the image and likeness of God. We live in the world, but we must never let it shape us in ways contrary to God's gifts of life and love.

✠ *What can I learn from this passage?*

The issue of resurrection (20:27–40)

That we will never cease to exist is an astounding thought. Faith in the resurrection is a central belief of Christianity, and for many, the desire to spend eternity with the loving God is a motive for living Jesus' Law as faithfully as possible.

✠ *What can I learn from this passage?*

The question about David's son (20:41—21:4)

Many of the religious leaders of Jesus' day may have been sincere in their desire to serve God, but some fell victim to their desire for recognition, honor, and intellectual superiority. That temptation exists down to our present day in the lives of some who are dedicated to God. Jesus calls us to remember that we are all servants, as Jesus was.

✠ *What can I learn from this passage?*

The beginning of the end (21:5–19)

Since Jesus' day, we have experienced many of the catastrophes predicted by Jesus, and the end has not yet come. The basic message is one we have heard often, "Be prepared, for you know not the day nor the hour."

✠ *What can I learn from this passage?*

PART 2: INDIVIDUAL STUDY (LUKE 21:20—22:53)

Day 1: The Great Tribulation (21:20–38)

Although Roman armies invaded and destroyed Jerusalem in 70, Luke, who is aware of the destruction, writes as though Jesus is predicting the destruction as a future event. Jesus warns that everyone in the city must flee and that those outside the city must not return to it. Jesus refers to the period of destruction as "days of vengeance," when everything written will take place. The time will be one of great tragedy. The pregnant and those who are nursing will suffer special hardship. Many will be killed; others will be taken captive. And Jerusalem will be destroyed by the Gentile (Roman) forces. The "times of the Gentiles," which Luke declares as something that must be fulfilled, seems to be a reference to the spread of the Gospel throughout the Gentile world.

Luke returns to his description of the end times with the use of apocalyptic language. The heavens will go through great changes in the sun, moon, and stars, and nations will experience confusion from the roaring of the seas and waves. The fear of some will be so great that they will die in frightened anticipation of what will come. The heavens will be shaken, and the Son of Man will come in great power and glory. When Luke speaks of "the Son of Man" in reference to Jesus in this passage, he is referring to the glorified Christ coming at the end of time. For those loyal to God, it is a moment of triumph when they will stand tall and rejoice that the time of their glorious redemption is about to take place.

Jesus draws a lesson from the fig tree, or any other tree. Luke, writing for an audience that might not be familiar with fig trees, adds the phrase "all the other trees." People can read the signs of the seasons from these trees, knowing that summer is near when the trees begin to bud. In the same way, Jesus tells his audience that they should also learn to read the signs of the times. When they see the events he foretells taking place, they should know that the time of fulfillment is near. The generation to which Jesus is speaking will not pass away until the destruction of Jerusalem. Jesus' words will continue into eternity.

Jesus warns his listeners not to be caught by surprise, entangled in the pleasures and cares of the world. The day of the Lord will come upon all suddenly, so all must be constantly on guard. They must pray to escape the wrath that is to come and to stand with the security of true discipleship before the Son of Man (Jesus as he comes in glory). While in Jerusalem, Jesus taught daily in the Temple and spent nights on the Mount of Olives. Early in the morning, Jesus continued his teachings in the Temple, where the people would rise early to listen to his message.

Lectio Divina

Spend 8 to 10 minutes in silent contemplation of the following passage:

> The continual theme of vigilance comes again. Be prepared! Jesus exhorts his listeners to pray for strength against tribulation and to stand firm. This exhortation from Jesus becomes sound advice for all of us, since we can all expect the day when our life on Earth will end, whether it be a day of catastrophe for creation or a day when the sun is shining and all is well in the world.

✠ *What can I learn from this passage?*

Day 2: The Plot to Kill Jesus (22:1–23)

The author relates Jesus' passion to his temptation in the desert. Luke tells us that when Jesus overcame the temptations in the desert, Satan "departed from him for a time" (4:13). The passion of Jesus becomes Satan's opportunity, beginning with a conspiracy against Jesus and concluding with his burial.

As Jesus sent his disciples to prepare for the Passover meal, Judas met with the chief priests and Temple guards to plot Jesus' betrayal. Although the feast of Passover was celebrated on the first day of the harvest feast of Unleavened Bread, lasting for seven days, these were considered separate feasts according to Jewish customs. Luke mistakenly identifies them as one feast. Luke states that Satan takes possession of Judas Iscariot, significantly referred to as "one of the Twelve," but like Matthew and Mark, he gives no motive for his betrayal. Judas goes to the priests and the temple guard, who offer Judas money for betraying Jesus, and Judas, accepting their offer, awaits an opportunity to hand him over at a time when crowds are absent.

In the meanwhile, Jesus sends Peter and John ahead to prepare the place for the meal. Luke follows Matthew and Mark in placing the Last Supper in the context of the Passover meal, the sacred meal of the Israelites celebrating their freedom from the slavery of Egypt and their new life in the Promised Land. He tells them they will encounter a man carrying a jar of water who will lead them to a house. They are to ask the master of the house for a guest room in which Jesus can celebrate the Passover with his disciples. The two disciples do as Jesus directed them, and they prepare for the Passover meal.

Up to this point in the Passion narrative, Luke has been following Mark, but he now adds material found only in his own tradition ("L"). At the supper, Jesus expresses how he has longed to eat this Passover with them before he suffers, declaring he would not eat it again until it is fulfilled in the kingdom of God. This fulfillment is most likely a reference to the era that begins with the resurrection of Jesus. Luke here clearly identifies the Last Supper with the Passover and sets it in the framework of the kingdom of God, where it will reach its fulfillment.

Jesus interrupts the flow of the Passover meal to offer his disciples his Body and Blood. He takes a cup, offers thanks, and directs his disciples to take it and share it among themselves. The Last Supper would continue with the future followers of Jesus. It is not clear that Jesus is referring to his eucharistic cup at this point, since he makes no mention of his blood at this point. After offering the cup to his disciples, he then takes the bread, blesses and breaks it, and gives it to them, saying, "This is my body, which will be given for you; do this in memory of me." After they have eaten, he takes the cup and declares that this is a cup of the new covenant in his blood "which will be shed for you." The eucharistic celebration found here is similar to the ritual found in Paul's First Letter to the Corinthians (11:23–26ff). Jesus directs his disciples to perform this ritual in memory of him. On the feast of the Passover, the blood of the lamb would be sprinkled on the altar. Jesus now becomes the new lamb who offers his blood as the new covenant that will be shed for all.

Jesus proclaims that the "betrayer" is at table with him, but he neither mentions Judas by name nor does he name him when the betrayer leaves the room. Jesus adds that although the Son of Man (the suffering servant) has come and will endure the suffering foretold by the prophets, the guilt of the one who betrays him is not lessened. The disciples debate who would perform such a deed. Luke omits their questioning of Jesus with the words, "Surely it is not I?" as found in Mark (14:19).

Lectio Divina

Spend 8 to 10 minutes in silent contemplation of the following passage:

> At the Last Supper, Jesus declares that he is giving his body and blood for our salvation. In Catholic belief, the Last Supper is still taking place in every eucharistic celebration. It is timeless and real, and a living memorial of Jesus' passion, death, resurrection, and ascension.

✠ *What can I learn from this passage?*

Day 3: A Dispute About the Greatest (22:24–38)

The disciples dispute among themselves which of them is the greatest. Matthew and Mark place this dispute at another time in their gospels (Matthew 20:25–28; Mark 10:42–45). Luke places it at the Last Supper, showing that the disciples, on the eve of the fulfillment of Jesus' ministry, still do not understand the meaning of the kingdom of God. Jesus tells them that he comes among them, not as one served at table, but as one who serves. He adds that they will sit on the thrones judging the twelve tribes of Israel. This is a reference to the new Israel that will replace the Israel of the Old Testament, which was built upon the twelve tribes of Israel. The disciples are a symbol of the new Israel. Jesus makes a reference to a meal, which is a sign that the time for the messianic banquet has arrived.

Jesus predicts that Simon Peter will deny him. He states that Satan sought to overcome Simon, but Jesus prayed for him that he may turn back and remain faithful. In this passage, when Peter boasts of his own strength in his willingness to accept imprisonment and death for Jesus, Jesus warns him that he will deny knowing Jesus three times before the cock crows.

Jesus recalls that he sent his disciples out in the past without money, supplies, or sandals and that they still lacked nothing on their journey. Using the symbols of a purse, a traveling bag, and a sword, he now warns them to prepare for the persecution ahead. When the disciples show that they have two swords, Jesus abruptly ends by saying it is enough, which seems to mean he has spoken enough for them to understand him, but unfortunately, they did not.

Lectio Divina

Spend 8 to 10 minutes in silent contemplation of the following passage:

> In an earlier passage in the gospels, Peter was able to walk on water when he kept his eye on Christ. But when he looked around at the storm, he began to sink. When Peter betrays Christ during the passion, he is looking at the dangers around him rather than keeping his thoughts on Jesus.

✠ *What can I learn from this passage?*

Day 4: Agonizing Events on the Mount of Olives (22:39–53)

Jesus and the disciples depart to their common camping area on the Mount of Olives where they rested during the feast. Jesus bids the disciples to pray so that they might not have to face the test, that is, the difficult struggles ahead. Luke, unlike the authors of the other gospels, does not have Jesus choose Peter, James, and John as companions during his passion in the garden. Jesus addresses all the disciples in the Gospel of Luke when he advises them to pray.

Jesus goes ahead a short distance to pray, and he prays alone for this cup of suffering to pass from him. He commits himself to the will of God. Luke alone speaks of the intense agony Jesus endures in the garden. The text does not tell us that Jesus sweat blood but that his sweat became so intense that it fell to the ground like drops of blood. When Jesus returns to his disciples, he finds them asleep. Luke, perhaps in defense of Jesus' disciples, adds that they were sleeping because of grief. Jesus urges them to pray that they may not have to be tested.

Judas leads the religious leaders to the Mount of Olives and the place where Jesus and his disciples stayed while in Jerusalem. As Judas attempts to kiss Jesus, Jesus asks if he is betraying the Son of Man with a kiss. In this passage, Jesus refers to himself as the Son of Man, understood here in the sense of the suffering servant found in the writings of the prophet Isaiah. When one of the followers of Jesus cuts off the ear of a servant of the high priest, Jesus orders his disciples to cease using their sword. Only in the Gospel of Luke do we read that Jesus touched the servant's ear and healed him.

The crowd that came out against Jesus seems to be an unlikely group. Luke names the high priests, the chiefs of the Temple, and the elders, who would most likely have preferred to remain at the Temple rather than come out openly armed to seize Jesus. Jesus asks why they came out under the cloak of darkness when they had other opportunities to take him when he was preaching in the Temple. In the Scriptures, evil and darkness are often aligned as one. Jesus tells them that this is the hour for the triumph of darkness, meaning the time when God allowed the power of evil to succeed.

Lectio Divina

Spend 8 to 10 minutes in silent contemplation of the following passage:

Evil casts its shadow across the narrative, as Judas, once a close friend of Jesus, attempts to betray him with a friendship kiss. Judas has joined the hypocritical ways of the scribes and Pharisees. God allows evil to have power in the world, but Jesus came to give us an example of confronting evil without letting evil shape us.

✠ *What can I learn from this passage?*

Review Questions

1. What do we learn from the fig tree?
2. What is the significance of Judas' betrayal of Jesus?
3. What does the disciples' argument about who is the greatest among them tell us about them?
4. What gave Peter the belief that he would be willing to die with Jesus?
5. What does the agony in the garden tell us about Jesus?

LESSON 10

Death and Resurrection of Jesus

LUKE 22:54—24:53

Thus it is written that the Messiah would suffer and rise from the dead on the third day and that repentance, for the forgiveness of sins, would be preached in his name to all the nations, beginning from Jerusalem (24:46–47).

Opening Prayer (SEE PAGE 14)

Context

Part 1: Luke 22:54—23:56 Jesus endures rejection during his passion in Peter's denials and the pain and humiliation inflicted by the religious leaders, Pilate, and Herod. The people call for Jesus' crucifixion while asking for the release of the notorious criminal Barabbas. Jesus carries his cross to the place known as the Scull, where he is crucified. Joseph of Arimathea buries Jesus' body.

Part 2: Luke 24:1–53 Luke speaks of the women at the empty tomb and the two men in dazzling clothes who announce Jesus' resurrection. Jesus appears to two men on the road to Emmaus who do not recognize him until evening when he breaks bread in their presence and vanishes from their sight. They rush to tell the others about Jesus' resurrection, but Jesus had already appeared to Simon. Jesus' disciples become witnesses of his ascension.

PART 1: GROUP STUDY (LUKE 22:54—23:56)

Read aloud Luke 22:54—23:56.

22:54–65 Peter's denial

As Jesus is led away to the house of the high priest, Peter follows at a distance. Luke immediately turns his attention to Peter in the courtyard and adds small details that heighten the denials of Peter. Peter denies knowing Jesus, he denies his relationship with the community of the Twelve, and even denies knowing anything about Jesus. At the third denial the cock crows, and Jesus turns to look at Peter. This look of Jesus at Peter is mentioned only in Luke's Gospel. When Jesus looks at Peter, Peter remembers Jesus' prediction that he would deny Jesus three times before the cock crows, and he leaves, weeping uncontrollably over his denial of Jesus.

In contrast to Peter, Jesus stands firm against his accusers. Before Jesus is brought before the Sanhedrin, the soldiers blindfold, slap, and taunt him. They ridicule him as a prophet, hinting at the accusation that will be leveled at him.

22:66–71 The trial of Jesus

Unlike Mark and Matthew, Luke does not mention Jesus being brought before the Sanhedrin for a trial during the night. By contrast, the trial in this gospel takes place at daybreak. When the Sanhedrin asks Jesus if he is the Messiah, he tells them of the futility of giving an answer. They refuse to listen to him or debate with him. Jesus refers to himself as the Son of Man, sitting at the place of highest honor (the right hand) of the Power of God. In this reference, "Son of Man" alludes to Jesus in his glory.

When they ask if Jesus is then the Son of God, Jesus replies that they are the ones who say that he is. It seems unlikely that they would have understood Jesus' acceptance of the title Son of God in the same way we understand it today. Luke, writing many years later, makes this claim of divinity the reason for the condemnation of Jesus.

23:1–25 Jesus before Pilate

When the religious leaders bring Jesus to Pilate, they change the accusation against him from blasphemy to undermining the nation. They falsely accuse him of telling the people they did not have to pay taxes to Rome. They also accuse him of calling himself the Messiah and a king. This last accusation is the one about which Pilate questions Jesus, asking if he is the king of the Jews. Jesus does not deny the title, saying that Pilate, not he, is the one saying it. Jesus and Pilate would understand the title in two different ways, since Jesus is referring to a spiritual kingdom while Pilate is speaking of a political kingdom.

Pilate announces to the crowds that he finds no fault in Jesus, but the religious leaders accuse Jesus of stirring up the people from Galilee to Jerusalem. At the mention of the name Galilee, Pilate sees his chance to rid himself of the responsibility of this judgment by sending Jesus to Herod, who is tetrarch of Galilee. During the time of a great feast, the rulers would also come to Jerusalem to be nearby in case trouble erupted. Both Pilate and Herod are in Jerusalem for the feast, so Pilate sends Jesus to Herod.

Luke told us earlier in his gospel that Herod, who had killed John the Baptist, wondered if Jesus were John raised from the dead. Now, with Jesus in his presence, Herod wants to be entertained by this miracle worker, hoping he would perform some miraculous sign for him. The religious leaders accuse Jesus before Herod. Herod and his guards mock Jesus, beat him, put a royal cloak on him, and send him back to Pilate. Ironically, Herod and Pilate, who had been enemies up to this point, now become friends.

Although Pilate in reality could hardly be called a compassionate man, he tries to persuade the religious leaders not to condemn Jesus. Luke lightens the role played by Rome in the execution of Jesus, perhaps due to the audience of Gentiles for whom he was writing. Pilate declares that neither he nor Herod find Jesus guilty of anything deserving of death, and he expresses his intent to free Jesus after flogging him.

The crowd cries out for the release of Barabbas, a rebel guilty of murder in a rebellion, and they call for the crucifixion of Jesus. In Mark's Gospel, Pilate gives the crowd a choice between freeing Jesus or Barabbas, but Luke makes no mention of Pilate giving the people a choice. He simply presents the crowd as crying out for the release of Barabbas. Three times Pilate attempts to free Jesus, claiming he has not found him guilty of any crime, but the crowd continues its uproar, and Pilate orders Jesus to be treated according to the will of the crowd. He releases Barabbas and hands Jesus over to the crowd to be treated as they wish. The crowds have already called for Jesus' crucifixion. The manner of Jesus' death placed him in the company of lowly criminals, rejected by his own people.

23:26–43 The way of the cross

Simon of Cyrene, although he is forced to carry the cross for Jesus, symbolically follows Jesus as a true disciple. Luke adds that many women mourned and lamented Jesus, thus pointing out that women were also disciples of Jesus. Jesus speaks to the women who come out to mourn, warning that they should not weep for him, but for themselves and their children. He predicts that the day of destruction will come when the people will struggle and suffer so greatly that they will consider the curse of bareness or being crushed under the hills as a blessing. If the Romans treat an innocent Jesus in such a manner (the green wood), how much more fierce will be their treatment of the guilty people of Jerusalem (the dry wood)?

Luke does not use the Hebrew name "Golgotha" as the place of crucifixion, but instead uses the name the "Skull," which describes the shape of the hill. The Gospel of Luke alone mentions Jesus' prayer of forgiveness for those responsible for putting him to death. This prayer is not found in most ancient manuscripts of Luke's Gospel, implying that the passage, although currently accepted as part of the inspired Scripture, may be an addition from a later editor. In accordance with an Old Testament prophecy, the soldiers gamble for his garments as the psalm says, "They divide my garments among them; for my clothing they cast lots" (22:19).

Although Luke mentions that people are standing around the cross, he only speaks of the religious leaders as ridiculing Jesus, mocking him, and challenging him to save himself if he is the Messiah of God. These words demonstrate their lack of understanding concerning the true meaning of Messiah. Luke has the guards refer to Jesus mockingly as the "king of the Jews," and they place an inscription over his head proclaiming that his crime was claiming to be the king of the Jews.

Luke alone recounts the story of the conversation between Jesus and the two criminals crucified with him. One of the criminals ridicules Jesus, challenging him to save himself and them if he is the Messiah. The other criminal, recognizing his sinfulness, rebukes him, declaring he should have fear of God at this condemnation to death, adding that they at least deserve this punishment for their crimes while Jesus has done nothing criminal. The repentant criminal then begs Jesus to remember him when he comes into his kingdom. Jesus responds that he will be with him this day in paradise. Paradise was understood to be that place of happiness and peace where the dead awaited the Final Judgment.

23:44–49 Jesus dies on the cross

Jesus is on the cross from midday (noon) until midafternoon (three o'clock), and Luke tells us that the sun did not shed its light during this period due to an eclipse of the sun. Jesus cries out in a loud voice words from Psalm 31:6, by which he commits his spirit to God and dies. The curtain in the Temple is torn in two, symbolizing the destruction of the old temple and the beginning of the new in Jesus himself. A centurion, instead of proclaiming that Jesus was truly the Son of God as found in the other synoptic gospels, declares that Jesus was truly an innocent man. The crowd reacts with humility and guilt, while the friends of Jesus and the women watch from a distance.

23:50–56 The burial of Jesus

Joseph, a man from Arimathea, a town north of Jerusalem arrives on the scene here. Although Joseph was a member of the Sanhedrin, he did not take part in the condemnation of Jesus. When he receives permission from Pilate to take the body of Jesus, he removes the body from the cross, wraps it in fine linen, and lays it in a new grave cut out of a rock. The urgency of the burial is explained by the simple statement that the Sabbath was about to begin. Women witness the burial of Jesus, noting the place of the tomb. With the approaching Sabbath, the women hasten home to prepare the usual spices and perfumes used for burials. Despite the Jews' rejection of Jesus, Luke shows the women continuing to follow the Mosaic Law of the Sabbath rest.

Review Questions

1. What does Peter's denial of Jesus teach us?
2. What happened at the trial of Jesus?
3. Why was Pilate intent on freeing Jesus?
4. What significant events took place during Jesus' way of the cross?

Closing Prayer (SEE PAGE 14)

Pray the closing prayer now or after *lectio divina*.

Lectio Divina (SEE PAGE 7)

Relax your body and maintain a posture of prayer (back straight, eyes shut, feet flat on the floor). This exercise can take as long as you want, but in the context of this Bible study, 10 to 20 minutes should be sufficient.

The meditations that follow are provided only to help group participants use this prayer form, but note that *lectio* is intended to bring one to a place of prayerful contemplation where the Word of God speaks to the hearer from his or her heart. (See page 7 for further instruction.)

Peter's denial (22:54–65)

When Peter realized he had betrayed Christ, he wept bitterly, and from that moment until the resurrection of Jesus, Peter's personal passion began. He had to live with himself, witnessing the passion of Jesus and being unable to reveal to Jesus his deep sorrow. This period in the courtyard would never be forgotten by Peter, even after he turned back to Jesus.

✠ *What can I learn from this passage?*

The trial of Jesus (22:66–71)

The confrontation Jesus faced was that they were questioning him with no intention of believing his answer, but with the intention of turning his answer against him. Jesus once said, "Let the one who has ears to hear, hear." It takes faith to understand and accept Jesus' message.

✠ *What can I learn from this passage?*

Jesus before Pilate (23:1–25)

In this darkest moment of the passion, the light of Christ is just a glimmer of light in the darkness. Jesus' disciples must accept that they appear to be just a glimmer in the darkness of evil in the world, but that glimmer can light up the world with the help of God, as happened when Jesus was raised from the dead.

✠ *What can I learn from this passage?*

The way of the cross (23:26–43)

Typically, Jesus does not think of himself on his journey to the cross as he directs the women not to weep for him, but to weep for those who will suffer during the Roman invasion. Right to the end on the cross, Jesus reveals the love of God for all, even sinners, when he declares, "Father, forgive them, for they know not what they do." In his last moments, Jesus offers forgiveness and hope to sinners.

✠ *What can I learn from this passage?*

Jesus dies on the cross (23:44–49)

Jesus' last act was to abandon himself to the loving hands of God the Father. In our living and our dying, we abandon ourselves to God's will, and the final act of abandoning our will to God comes when we commend our spirit to the Lord in death. We abandon ourselves to God with trust that we shall meet with an eternal reward as Jesus promised.

✠ *What can I learn from this passage?*

The burial of Jesus (23:50–56)

Jesus' life on Earth has come to an end. After the women viewed the place of Jesus' burial, they returned home, and the silence of the Sabbath rest pervades the story and the mood of the Church on Holy Saturday. Holy Saturday is a time to reflect on all the gifts that come to us because Jesus became human and lived in our midst.

✠ *What can I learn from this passage?*

PART 2: INDIVIDUAL STUDY (LUKE 24:1–53)

Day 1: The Empty Tomb (24:1–12)

Here, Luke speaks of the events surrounding the resurrection of Jesus. He presents a more lengthy narrative than those found in the other synoptic gospels. We learn from Luke that the Messiah had to suffer his passion and death in order to enter into his glory. It is the conquest of death that delivers total salvation.

In the Gospel of Luke, three women come to the tomb to complete the burial rites for Jesus. When they arrive at the tomb, they find the stone rolled back. They enter there, but do not find the body of Jesus.

Luke names Mary Magdalene, Joanna, and Mary the mother of James as three of the women who come to the tomb. Luke alone names Joanna as one of the women present at the tomb. The women see two men there, who tell them they should not look for the living among the dead. They remind the women that Jesus himself foretold his passion, death, and resurrection. The three women carry the message of the two men to the disciples. There are several differences in the empty-tomb stories found in the gospels. Luke tells us that two men in dazzling clothes (a reference to heavenly garments) speak to the women. Mark has one man greet them, Matthew has an angel, and John has two angels.

Unlike Mark and Matthew, who tell of Jesus going into Galilee, Luke follows the Gospel of John and places Jesus' resurrection ministry in Jerusalem. Luke, the author of the Acts of the Apostles, will tell how faith in Jesus moved from Jerusalem to other areas of the world. He, like John, adds the story of Peter rushing off to the tomb after hearing the words of the women. His reaction shows how unexpected the resurrection of Jesus was to the Apostles, despite the predictions of Jesus. The women and Peter are given as witnesses to the empty tomb.

Lectio Divina

Spend 8 to 10 minutes in silent contemplation of the following passage:

> The paschal mystery continues as Jesus moves through his passion and death to his resurrection and ascension. Paul reminds us that through Christ's death and resurrection, we attain salvation. He writes that "just as Christ was raised from the dead by the glory of the Father, we too might live in newness of life" (Romans 6:4). The empty tomb teaches that the mission of Christ did not end with his death.

✠ *What can I learn from this passage?*

Day 2: The Disciples on the Road to Emmaus (24:13–35)

The gospel writer provides vivid details about the two people on the road to Emmaus. The two are returning home from Jerusalem when Jesus, whom they do not recognize, joins them on their journey. Luke implies that they did not have the faith necessary to recognize Jesus. Many of the Resurrection narratives begin with this lack of recognition when Jesus appears to his disciples. Only after Jesus speaks with them are they able to recognize him as Jesus the Lord.

Cleopas, who may have been known to the members of the early Church community, tells Jesus, the stranger, how they had hoped that Jesus was the great prophet who would be the one to save the nation. He lays the blame for the death of Jesus completely on the shoulders of the Jewish leaders, with no mention of the part played by the Roman rulers. He adds that some women brought disturbing news earlier in the day about an empty tomb and a vision of angels who told them that Jesus was alive. Cleopas adds that the day was the "third day," not realizing this was the day of resurrection predicted by Jesus.

Jesus chides the two for their inability to understand that the Scriptures had predicted this passage as the way to true Messiahship. On the journey, Jesus had explained all the Scriptures referring to him, and how he had to pass through all these things to enter his glory. As they near Emmaus, the two disciples urge Jesus to stay with them since it is almost evening.

Luke describes the meal as a eucharistic meal in which Jesus takes the bread, blesses it, breaks it, and gives it to them. When they receive the bread, they recognize Jesus, who disappears from their midst. Only then do they recall the effect the words of Jesus had on them during their journey to Emmaus. They immediately return to Jerusalem with their good news. Upon their arrival, in the midst of the Eleven and other disciples, they learn that the Lord has appeared to Simon. They then tell the other disciples how they had recognized Jesus in the "breaking of the bread," an expression used in the early Church for the eucharistic celebration.

Lectio Divina

Spend 8 to 10 minutes in silent contemplation of the following passage:

> Jesus continues to live with us in the Eucharist. His disciples recognized the resurrected Jesus in the "breaking of the bread," which is the Eucharist. Every time we share in Eucharist, we can exclaim that the Lord has been raised and lives among us.

✠ *What can I learn from this passage?*

Day 3: Jesus Appears to His Disciples and Ascends (24:36–53)

When Jesus appears to the disciples and greets them with the usual Jewish greeting of "Peace," he invites them to look at the wounds in his hands and feet, thus proving he is the same Jesus who was crucified and has now been raised. He invites them to touch him and know that he is not a ghost, and as a last sign that he has been raised, Jesus eats in their presence. Jesus tells the disciples to recall his words and the words of the Law, the prophets, and the psalms concerning him. Through Jesus' resurrection, the disciples are able to understand the meaning of the Scriptures.

The disciples are to be witnesses to Jesus, beginning at Jerusalem and reaching out to the whole world. Jesus alludes to the sending of the Spirit when he tells his disciples that he will send them the promise of God. They are to remain in Jerusalem until they are clothed with power from God. The resurrection and ascension of Jesus appear to take place on the same day in the gospel, whereas the Acts of the Apostles (1:3-9) describes the ascension as taking place forty days later. In reality, the resurrection and

---

ascension took place at the same instant, because Jesus' glory consisted in his exaltation, that is, his ascension.

Jesus leads the disciples out to Bethany, blesses them, and is taken into heaven. The disciples pay homage to Jesus in recognition of his divinity and then return in joy to Jerusalem and the Temple, where they teach Jesus' message. The gospel has come full circle, beginning with the appearance of the angel to Zechariah in the Temple and ending with the disciples of Jesus preaching in the Temple. We now arrive at the doorstep of the Acts of the Apostles, which will explain how the message of Jesus moves out from Jerusalem to all nations.

Lectio Divina

Spend 8 to 10 minutes in silent contemplation of the following passage:

Jesus, who suffered and died, has now become our wounded healer. The wounded healer gives his followers an example of the reward that awaits all those wounded for love of God. He blesses his disciples and is taken into heaven. The mission of Jesus now becomes the mission of Christianity.

✠ *What can I learn from this passage?*

Review Questions

1. What does the empty tomb teach us?
2. What is significant about Jesus' appearance on the road to Emmaus?
3. What does touching and eating have to do with Jesus' resurrection?
4. Where does the preaching of the Good News begin according to Jesus? Why?
5. How does the resurrection of Jesus affect your life?